GENUINELY SEEKING WORK
MASS UNEMPLOYMENT ON MERSEYSIDE IN THE 1930s

by

Sam Davies, Pete Gill, Linda Grant, Martyn Nightingale, Ron Noon, and Andy Shallice

Members of Merseyside Socialist Research Group

First published 1992 by by Liver Press, 1 & 3 Grove Road, Rock Ferry, Birkenhead, Wirral, Merseyside, L42 3XS

Typeset by Northern Writers, 77 Marford Crescent, Sale, Cheshire M33 4DN
Printed by Birkenhead Press Limited, 1-3 Grove Road, Rock Ferry, Birkenhead, Merseyside L42 3XS

ISBN 1 871201 04 7

CONTENTS

Dedication

As this book reached its final stages, we heard of the death of Frank Banton. This came as a shock to all of us who knew him.

Frank was fond of referring to himself as an "ordinary fella". Perhaps he was – but his "ordinariness" was very special. His life was a tribute to many who, like him, have spent their lives struggling for socialism.

Frank came from Cumbria, but he made his home in Liverpool, a city he came to love and depend on. A city he could never leave: in fact he often talked of how he would be lost without it. Yet in his deep attachment to the place, he was never insular. He was one of the first to recognise the importance of international contacts among trade unionists. Particularly so in the motor industry, where Frank spent almost twenty years of his life, as a worker and trade union representative, first at Standards, then at Fords.

Eventually, Frank's militancy and the Thatcherite "economic miracle" cost him his job. However, being Frank, he looked for a way to struggle on, and he found it – Liverpool Polytechnic. There, thirsting for knowledge, he read books, wrote essays, organised meetings and generally shook things up.

Frank lived a full life, and his concern to fight for the underdog led him up many avenues. He became a film star once (working with Jim Allen on *The Rank and File*). He held a variety of positions within the T & G, and eventually became a sociologist. But while his heart remained with the union, he found new challenges. He acted as a consultant on academic research projects; he worked with political refugees; he got involved in a number of tenants' campaigns. Throughout all of this, his interest in the underdog remained. Frank genuinely wanted to help. He wanted things to be better in this world. He was always looking for solutions.

Raymond William has written of how a labour movement needs to employ and develop resources for hope. In so many ways, Frank's life embodied such hope. In this he was a man to admire and remember. Frank Banton was no "ordinary fella" to those of us who were privileged to know and love him.

This book is dedicated to Frank and his hope and vision of a better future.

Preface

As this preface is written the new, gentler, more caring prime minister insists that the economy is experiencing a 'downturn', while exalted economists debate whether the UK is diving into a 'depression' or 'merely a recession'. This serves to remind us why we set out to research and write this book. During the discussions and debate which we had following the publication in 1980 of *Merseyside in Crisis*, we were frequently struck by the comparisons people made between Merseyside's situation then and during the nineteen-thirties. A number of themes seemed to recur: mass unemployment, certainly, but also the state's primary concern with reducing public expenditure and local authorities consequently finding themselves squeezed between the state's pressure on the one hand, and local political pressure to maintain services on the other.

So we decided to look more carefully at the experiences of Merseyside during the nineteen-thirties. As we did so a number of factors became apparent which are major features of the discussion in this book. First, the eighties were a time when people's history was in danger of falling victim to the heritage industry's 'disneyfication' of the past and it seemed important to us to place on record people's real sufferings. Secondly, and related to the first point, was that people's perceptions of the thirties were coming increasingly from professional historians, many of whom wrote their history from 'above' – from the perspective of states and employers. Some of this work, indeed, now presents the thirties as a decade of progress in economic 'restructuring' and 'adjustment' – euphemisms which conceal the real damage to people's lives as do others like 'collateral damage' in 1991. We felt it important to reinforce the alternative perspective – that from 'below'. Thirdly, we have tried to indicate that some of the strongest images of the thirties are themselves based on a partial interpretation of the time. For example, the image of unemployment affecting predominantly the white working class male is shown to be distorted and we have attempted to show how the deprivations of the thirties affected more particularly women, blacks and young people.

In presenting our findings we have given priority to making them accessible to the people of Merseyside and indicating to people where they might go for further information. This is not intended to be an academic book, but we have made reference to some of the academic debates about the period where we thought it appropriate. Apart from those writings already published on the period, the main sources we consulted were the local press, the reports of official and unofficial bodies, and the minutes of local authorities. Also we interviewed a number of local people – we do not present their views as necessarily 'representative' of all opinions at the time, but in order to illustrate people's experiences.

Our discussion follows a similar structure to that of *Merseyside in Crisis* in which we, first, examined the roots of the crisis in the actions of capital and the state, and, second, considered the working class response. In 1980 we had no need to tell the people of Merseyside what life was like because they were living it, but in this discussion of the thirties Part One describes in some detail who were the unemployed and the conditions in which they lived. In Part Two we discuss the policies and actions during the period of the state and the ruling class. In particular, we examine the succession of unemployment benefit regulations introduced as the state struggled to 'balance the books' during the crisis and also the new policies introduced by employers so that those in work could not escape its consequences. In Part Three we examine how the working class responded to the conditions and policies discussed in the first two parts. As might be expected, given the evidence of divisions between people in their experience of the crisis, the response was mixed – sometimes hesitant but hopeful, sometimes defiant but divided. Perhaps the most divisive response was that associated with Orangeism and Fascism. The unions' and the Labour Party's response was more hesitant than reactionary, except when it was associated with sectarianism, while the most hopeful and defiant response often came from the National Unemployed Workers' Movement.

We have not attempted to draw up any particular set of 'lessons' that we believe should be taken from the thirties; rather, we have attempted to provide the people of Merseyside with the raw material, and some ideas which we hope will help them better to understand both the continuities and discontinuities of unemployment and deprivation on Merseyside.

All of the following people helped us: some provided their recollections of the thirties, others read and commented on earlier drafts. We thank them all for their time and trouble: Joseph Cleary, Jerry Dawson, Frank Deegan, Leon Davies, John Emmerson, John Hamilton, Harry Holmes, George Hughes, Ann Kelly, Nev Kirk, Harry Livermore, John McDermott, Jim Mottram, Bill Regan, Margaret Simey, Eric Taplin, Cath Terry, Billy Weaver, and Ted Williams.

We would welcome any comments that you might have on the book – the group can be contacted at the School of Social Science, John Moores University, Trueman Building, Webster Street, Liverpool L3 2ET.

March 1991

PART ONE
UNEMPLOYED LIVES

1
THE ROOTS OF THE CRISIS

"STAMPEDE FOR WORK
2,000 men for 500 jobs at
Mersey Dock

More than 2000 dockers stampeded for work at the Gladstone dock yesterday when the White Star liner *Baltic* was due to berth from New York with a miscellaneous cargo of 7000 tons. The *Baltic* was the first big liner with a large cargo to arrive for more than a week, and the prospect that additional overtime would be required to enable the vessel to make a quick turn around so that she would be able to leave on Saturday attracted a record number of dockers. The men began to form up before the vessel reached the landing stage and by one o'clock about 2,000 dockers waited to be picked up for duty. Only about 500 were required, however, and when the foremen appeared and called out certain men, the crowd stampeded. Police reinforcements were called and the stand was reformed while a further batch of men was chosen, but the ranks broke again and the foremen postponed the signing on till later in the day when the men were taken on and the work proceeded." *Liverpool Daily Post*, 11.3.1931.

Dockers and seafarers are traditionally viewed as the heart and soul of the Liverpool working class. The above description, even when allowances has been made for journalistic hyperbole, serves as a shocking reminder that in the frantic search for jobs and employment, people can behave like frightened animals, rushing impulsively to the call stand or the now infamous dockers' pen. It evokes powerfully and dramatically an era of mass unemployment and endemic underemployment for thou-

Photo 1: Six o'clock in the morning, February 1930, and men queue outside the dock sheds in Liverpool, desperately hoping to be taken on for work. Twice a day, every day, this was the reality of the casual system.

8

sands of Merseyside workers. 'Giz a job', the plaintive demand of Yosser Hughes in the fictionalised world of Alan Bleasdale's 1981 *Boys from the Blackstuff*, was in the historic year 1931 articulated woefully by the 2,000 that cried out when the *Baltic* docked in the river Mersey, and by many hundreds of thousands throughout what was left of the Devil's decade.

> "The life of everyone who lived through the years between 1914 and 1945 was likely to be scarred by two great memories: war and unemployment. These were not the only formative events in the first half of the twentieth century; but they affected the lives of more people, either directly or indirectly, than at any other time in English history."[1]

Two world wars delineate the period but not the main theme of this book. Millions were scarred by the experience of both wars. Hundreds of thousands were slaughtered in the trenches, bombing devastated whole cities, and conscription, evacuation and rationing affected all. Yet paradoxically the two world wars were periods of full employment, while the years between, years of peace, were years of mass unemployment. The memories and experience of unemployment are the main concerns of this book, but any analysis of the period has to be informed by the knowledge that it took World War Two, not a change in Government attitude or policy, to temporarily solve the problem of unemployment.

Capitalist Crisis
The end of the First World War, far from ushering in a return to economic growth, marked the beginning of a long phase of stagnation. It was a period characterised by recurrent economic crises and class conflict. Long waves of stagnation and expansion are endemic to industrial capitalism, and the post-1945 transition from a period of fast and, indeed, unprecedented growth to one of relative stagnation by the 1970s proves that history can repeat itself under conditions of advanced capitalism. Specific circumstances differentiate phases of capitalist development, but the recurring theme is whether and how the capitalist class can recreate the conditions for renewed long term expansion. Capital accumulation depends on the rate of profit and anything which raises this stimulates accumulation. An obvious way to secure the conditions for accumulation is to restore profits at the expense of the working class.

> "Whilst capitalist recovery has been brought about by a different combination of factors in each period, mass suffering on a truly vile scale has been a necessary part of the process every time."[2]

Mass unemployment and wage cuts were unquestionably the major weapons in that process in the years between the wars.

Within this context of capitalist crisis the state also plays a role by attempting to establish the framework for increasing profitability. In the first place, during the nineteen-twenties successive governments saw the way to achieve this as being by means of deflationary measures aimed at returning to pre-1914 conditions and, at the same time, attacking the strength and organisation of the trade unions, culminating in the defeat of the General Strike in 1926. Equally important, especially in the subsequent decade, the state used its legislative powers and influence to hasten the process of capital accumulation. It encouraged mergers, takeovers and rationalisation with a view to increasing the profitability of both traditional and newly expanding industries.

From 1920 the City, the Bank of England and their Treasury allies in Government, moved decisively to institutionalise their influence over economic policy. The epitome of this was the commitment to get back on to the international gold standard, the symbol of a pre-war era of world dominance by the City. The adherence to this international payments system was to prove disastrous, both intensifying mass unemployment and at the same time making it more difficult to pursue active policy measures to deal with it. In the light of subsequent exhortations by bankers, Treasury officials and politicians for workers to take the "medicine" of deflation and rising unemployment, an essential concomitant of gold standard policies, it is significant that Lloyd George found immediate return politically unacceptable in 1919. Faced with the special problems of demobilisation and the raised expectations of those who had been intensively exploited on the Western and Home fronts, ritual genuflections to economic and financial "orthodoxy" were less important than winning "the social peace". Once that critical threshold had been successfully crossed, an essentially bankers' and financiers' policy was single-mindedly pursued by Governments. Ironically the two minority Labour Governments of 1924 and 1929 were hooked on this paralysing economic orthodoxy.

Although the actual timing of the decision to return to gold was April 1925, the policy of "gold, sweat and tears" for the working class actually stretched from 1920 right down to 1931 when Britain was literally forced off the standard. Its consequences were grim and it is worth quoting John Maynard Keynes, the contemporary critic who more than anyone else highlighted the "waste" and social cost of it all:

"Credit restriction is an incredibly powerful instrument, and even a little of it goes a long way – especially where the opposite course is called for. The policy of deliberately intensifying unemployment with a view to forcing wage reductions is already partly in force, and the tragedy of our situation lies in the fact that, from the misguided stand-point which has been officially adopted, this course is theoretically justifiable. No section of labour will readily accept lower wages merely in response to sentimental speeches, however genuine by Mr. Baldwin. We are depending for the reduction of wages on the pressure of unemployment and of strikes and lockouts, and in order to make sure of this result we are deliberately intensifying the unemployment."[3]

At the patently unrealistic parity of $4.86 to the pound, sterling was overvalued, adversely affecting export industries. Even when there were signs, up to 1929, that other economies were expanding, the British economy remained in the doldrums. The price of maintaining the level of the pound was continued deflationary policies and high interest rates. Crucially policy was geared towards prices and exchange rates, rather than the real economic variables of output and employment. Unemployment was the "one absolute evil" which the Gold Standard medicine guaranteed.

Rewriting History

The Wall Street Crash of 1929 plunged the already weak British economy into the abyss of the thirties. By 1932 nearly one quarter of the working population were out of work and even in 1938 more than 2 million people were still unemployed. This was indeed the "devil's decade". Yet to many right wing historians and commentators of today the image of hunger marches, the criticisms of Government and Government policies, is misleading and supposedly too one-sided a view. From the viewpoint of the working class who bore the brunt of those policies, however, there was only one response – despair and anger at the sheer waste of those two decades. They would hardly have been appeased by the views of one economic historian who argued that,

"Despite the blackspots in the inter-war economy, notably the stagnation in exports and the heavy unemployment, economic growth was by no means negligible."[4]

The same historian also tells us that,

> "It would be profitable if scholars in future devoted more attention to the factors underlying this growth pattern rather than discussing the economic disasters which characterise the period."

In fact the years between the two wars, and the thirties in particular, have been interpreted and reinterpreted by professional historians to the extent that the very real experience of mass unemployment and misery that we document in this book has been considerably downgraded. Converts to a newer way of thinking suggest that it was the very pervasiveness of the image of the "hungry thirties" which camouflaged the supposedly more constructive and substantial achievements of those years. Alongside the decline of the older staple export industries, we are told, came the growth of new consumer goods and retail industries. Supposedly therefore Britain was looking much more like a modern twentieth century economy by 1939, and this meant a "respectable" overall growth performance and rising living standards for the majority who remained in work. The fact is that a process of restructuring of the economy was taking place which, under capitalism, is always patchy and uneven, both socially and geographically. The inter-war years were no exception and the bitter and gloomy images of the period have, we would argue, a much greater resonance. As one writer expressed it

> "The acrid fog of anxiety was the atmosphere which men and women breathed during a generation. Its effect cannot be statistically measured but equally it cannot be left out of any account of those years."[5]

Moreover, calculations of rising living standards for those in employment often fail to assess the extent of casual, semi-casual and seasonal work which made insecurity a fact of life for millions. On Merseyside the extent of casualism and seasonality of employment made life particularly insecure. Paradoxically official thinking in the thirties on the 'new' problem of unemployment was almost wholly connected with the unemployed miners of the Rhondda and cotton workers of Lancashire, and of the staple industries in general. It could be argued that Liverpool was given the by-pass not just in terms of manufacturing, but in terms of official recognition of its serious structural problems. Why was Merseyside not designated as a depressed area when legislation was passed in 1934? Making comparisons between competing "industrial graveyards" is an invidious exercise, but officially Merseyside wasn't even in the frame.

Merseyside in the Depression

Turning to the impact of the depression locally, by 1920 Merseyside, like many other regions, had experienced serious economic decline. In an international economy dislocated by the effects of war and a shrinkage of world trade, the region's prospects for recovery and growth were bleak. The run-down of Liverpool from a major commercial metropolis to what we described in *Merseyside in Crisis* as an unwanted mausoleum dates from this period.

The obvious structural problem for Merseyside was its dependence on the port and its activities, a position which had hardly altered by the outbreak of war in 1939. It was a lop-sided local economy over-dependent upon the service sector. The service industries employed nearly two thirds of the total insured workforce in 1932 compared with about a third nationally. The shipping, transport and distributive trades alone represented very nearly a half of local employment, while manufacturing industry was correspondingly under-represented, providing only 27% of jobs in the area.[6] The relative absence of factory type work was in direct contrast to most other industrial centres.

The vulnerability of the local economy to a decline in its service and manufacturing specialisms and to a slump in international trade was seriously exposed in the inter-war period. Total insured employment in Merseyside declined between 1924 and 1932 by 21% in transport, 25% in commerce, 33% in river and dock services, 39% in railways and by over a half in shipbuilding and repair.[7] In 1932, the worst year of the depression, unemployment locally totalled 108,000, a rate of 28% – nearly one in three of local workers.[8]

The more 'optimistic' national image of the thirties drawn recently by some historians bears no relation to Merseyside's actual experience in the decade. World trade declined more rapidly than world production: in the wake of trade and payments difficulties various countries turned to national solutions so that, by 1932, quotas, exchange controls and bilateral trading agreements had been established in an attempt to protect individual economies. The net effect of the thirties version of import controls was to particularly hinder export-orientated economies like Britain's. Being so dependent on the export trade, the port of Liverpool remained depressed. External circumstances were affecting the volume of shipping using the port, circumstances that were obviously beyond the control of Merseyside. Of course, that argument applied to the rest of the British economy, and particularly to other big ports, but the effects of the depression hit the Port of Liverpool hardest of all.

Part of the explanation for Liverpool suffering more than most ports can be found in the changing relationship between imports and exports and the fall in the volume of sea-borne passenger traffic in these years. In the inter-war years the ratio of exports to imports altered, with exports falling sharply as a proportion of British trade. Liverpool as the main export port was hardest hit. At the same time the operating costs of the port increased overall as ships still had to sail even though there had been a serious drop in cargoes carried. The passenger trade to the USA and Canada also declined, and this trade overall was beginning to shift to Southampton, with its convenient position relative to London and the Continent. So while trade overall was down in these years, the effects in Liverpool were compounded by the fact that Liverpool was losing, on average, 1% of its trade a year to other British ports. In the depths of the depression, in 1931, the overall volume of trade through Liverpool was only 42% of the 1924 figure – a catastrophic fall with implications for the wider local economy. By contrast Southampton had retained 72% of its trade over the same period, London 73% and Manchester 48%.[10] Behind the statistics were the grim experiences of those who were forced to fight for what limited work was available.

The marked fall in the export of cotton piece goods and the concomitant fall in imports of raw cotton was both important and symbolic since much of the prosperity of nineteenth century Liverpool had been based on this trade. In the thirties there was extra business generated from imports of cheap foodstuffs and raw materials, proving a bonus for many British ports, but it was not one enjoyed locally – the low value trade that the slump made more important was going elsewhere. As Liverpool continued to specialise in handling facilities for liners and in the export of high value manufactured goods, by 1938 Liverpool's share of total U.K. trade had fallen from a third to a fifth.

Such 'recovery' as there was nationally in the nineteen-thirties was characterised by the expansion of the 'new' industries aimed at the home market, a development which was especially evident in the relatively more prosperous Midlands and South. Structural alterations in the local economy were slight and consequently the area was for the most part by-passed in terms of growth industries. Liverpool's traditional infrastructural advantages were less relevant to those industries and the depression deepened. In 1934, Professor Caradog Jones of Liverpool University concluded in a survey of the region that it was 'beyond reasonable hope' to absorb the existing unemployed within ten years.[12] Liverpool's subsequent economic history suggests that the Professor was an optimist.

Notes
1. J.F.C. Harrison, *The Common People* (London, Fontana, 1984), p.348.
2. A. Friend & A. Metcalf, *Slump City: The Politics of Mass Unemployment* (London, Pluto Press, 1981), p.36.
3. Quoted in S. Pollard, *The Gold Standard and Employment Policies Between the Wars* (London, Methuen, 1970), p.36
4. D.H. Aldcroft & H.W. Richardson, *The British Economy 1870-1939* (London, Macmillan, 1969), p.6; D.H. Aldcroft, "Economic Growth in the Inter-War Years: A Reassessment", *Economic History Review*, Vol.XX, No.2, 1967, p.325.
5. E.J. Hobsbawm, *Industry and Empire* (London, Weidenfeld & Nicolson, 1968), p.176.
6. D. Caradog Jones, *Social Survey of Merseyside* (Liverpool, Liverpool University Press, 1934), Vol. II, pp.2-3.
7. Caradog Jones, Vol. II, p.52.
8. Caradog Jones, Vol. II, p.366.
9. Caradog Jones, Vol. II, pp.78-9.
10. Caradog Jones, Vol. II, p.63.
11. *Liverpool Daily Post*, 11.3.1931.
12. Caradog Jones, Vol. II, p.403.

2
WHO WERE THE UNEMPLOYED OF THE 1930s?

Most of us have an image in our minds of life in the nineteen-thirties. For some it springs from their own memories. For others it has been built on old newsreels, the stories of relatives and friends, or pictures in books. All but the least imaginative agree that it was a period characterised above all by the despair and suffering of many millions of people. But until recent years it was an image which required no clear definition. The passage of time had blurred the edges. Even by the nineteen-fifties the slogan 'ask your father', the rallying cry of post-war British politics, suggested that mass unemployment in the thirties was to be remembered only in so far as it 'reminded' people of how good their lives were now. But twenty years later comparisons between 'then and now' were being redrawn. Posters appeared on the theme, 'No Return to the 30s', with a picture which for many of us encapsulated our vision of the inter-war years: the Wigan miner, standing on a street corner, a sad, gaunt and hungry man. It seemed to say it all.

But this is too simplistic a picture. It evokes the human tragedy of the thirties but tells only half the story. It is an image which suggests that unemployment then was essentially a Northern and regional problem affecting an undifferentiated mass of white, male workers from the coalfields and shipyards; that the division in the working class was between the employed workers of the South and the Midlands and the forgotten unemployed of the North, Scotland, and Wales.

The other enduring image of the nineteen-thirties is that of the hunger march behind the Jarrow banner. Unemployed men, marching side by side demanding work not dole. Implicit in this image is the idea that the fight for the right to work was a clear political issue. The enemy was obvious and the unemployed were united in knowing who they were fighting and what they were fighting for.

But these images romanticise and simplify the past. They support a view which accepts the importance of sex, race, age, skill and locality in dividing the unemployed of today but fails to find an echo in the past. In

Photos 2 & 3: (2) The Jarrow Crusade and (3) the Wigan miner – two familiar images of the thirties, but they only tell part of the story.

this book we show that similar divisions were as significant and as politically crucial in the thirties. If we fail to recognise this we underestimate the obstacles confronted by political activists in the past, we avoid evaluating their experience and, perhaps more importantly, we disregard the continuity of political weaknesses within the working class movement which arise on the basis of these divisions.

'You Used to Fight for Work'

In April, 1929 the Liverpool Daily Post reported a 'disturbance' at Wapping Dock, Liverpool. At eight o'clock in the morning 500 men turned up at the dock in an attempt to get work on the fruit steamer *S.S. Scottish Prince*. There were only 200 jobs on the ship and when the timekeeper arrived to select them fighting broke out as men surged forward to reach the front of the queue. Within minutes some men lay injured and the police had been called in . The crowd were shouting, "we want work" and "remember our families!" as they lifted the timekeeper off his feet and pushed him along the quayside. Eventually 200 men were chosen, "preference being given to those out of work longest and those with large families".[1] Incidents such as this were to recur on Merseyside throughout the inter-war years, as we have already seen.

In the summer of 1932, 140,000 men and women were unemployed on Merseyside. In addition, another 90,000 could find work for only a few days each week.[2] Massive unemployment went hand in hand with the irregularity of work in a large number of local industries, creating a vast group of people whose standard of living was little different from that of the permanently unemployed. The crisis attacked the very heart of the local economy centred on the port. Thousands of dockers and seafarers, shipbuilders, and warehouse workers, clerks and porters were thrown out of work. Thousands more jostled on the stands along the Dock Road for a few days work here, a few days there. In 1936, the unemployment rate in Liverpool was 26% – twice the national average.[3]

Of course unemployment was nothing new to local workers. Merseyside had never offered guaranteed, permanent jobs. Just as dockers were taken on by the half day and seafarers by the voyage, so women in the food factories and tailoring workshops were employed for a week, a month or a season. But this long experience of insecurity was magnified by the depression. Work became more irregular and the pool of long term unemployed grew daily.

Dock workers were by far the most conspicuous section of the unemployed. In 1932 there were 30,000 registered dockers on Merseyside but in the same year nearly half of them were unemployed. Few found a full week's work in the thirties. The lucky ones worked for three days and signed on for the rest of the week. Others turned up at the stands in vain hope that their luck was in, that today the foreman would touch their shoulder and they would be taken on. All unemployed dockers had to attend the morning and midday stand every day in order to remain eligible for the dole. It was a demoralising experience with no guarantees.

"You used to fight for work. Oh, you fought for your work, no doubt about it, don't let anybody kid you otherwise. You fought for your job and especially a ship starting and there was going to be any value about – if there was going to be any money earned on it – the men fought to get it...Once you were employed, you weren't necessarily employed for a full day. The boss would come to you at ten to twelve, or a quarter to twelve and say, 'that will do', or 'clear out'. They weren't as polite as that, they'd just say, 'clear out there' and you had to go."[4]

As well as the loading and unloading of ships, there were a hundred and one jobs which relied on the activity of the port. With the port's decline ripples of unemployment spread across the city. The massive warehouses and storerooms required fewer and fewer workers. Carters, storekeepers, porters and messengers joined the ranks of the unemployed. And in turn, many of the pubs, cafes and shops along the Dock Road closed their doors for the last time.

The shipping lines, too, with their grand offices around the Pier Head, were to enter a phase of intense competition and rationalisation which saw many companies swallowed up and their headquarters transferred to London. In 1932 there were 5000 unemployed clerks on Merseyside.[5] Since the end of the First World War, 6,000 clerical jobs had been lost in the shipping industry alone. It was male clerks who were more likely to lose their jobs, since women's wages were normally half those of men and women had learnt to operate the new machinery which had been introduced into offices, especially the typewriter. Whilst in the thirties the number of women clerical workers, especially young single women, was slowly increasing, there were still almost twice as many male clerks. But many offices were subject to the casualism central to the local labour market. Some were run entirely by temporary staff, liable to be dismissed at a moment's notice. Clerks, bookkeepers, typists and secretaries joined the hopeless scramble for jobs.

In the winter of 1932-33, nearly half of the 34,400 workers in the shipping industry on Merseyside were unemployed. It was seafarers who were hardest hit. Already used to long periods of unemployment between voyages, for some the gap now stretched into years. The testimony of a Liverpool seafarer at the time bears witness to the crisis in the industry.

"Looking for a ship is neither a joy ride or a honeymoon. There are 13 miles of docks we are told by the Overhead Railway advert. The seaman looking for a ship has to keep his eyes not only upon these 13 miles of docks, but also upon that broad expanse of water called the River Mersey. He must also be a close student of the columns of the Journal of Commerce. He must not forget to note those ships that are paying off because the 'crowd may be going home'. He must know how the tides are running. He must be in and around the docks 24 hours a day, seven days a week, that is, if he is to find a ship with someone short. And it often occurs that when he gets a job it is one at short notice and he has to go away 'schooner rigged' with all the added discomforts which that implies.

On Tuesdays and Thursdays, Wednesdays and Fridays, he has to converge on Canning Place, where he lines up in front of a large board which bears the inscription of 'Ministry of Labour, Liverpool Seamen's Employment Exchange'. There are at present, 6700 seamen 'exchanging' their jobs ... Owing to the raising of the load line, the installation of diesel engines, the burning of oil instead of coal – in short, that rationalisation of shipping, together with knocking half a dozen companies into one, ships crews are getting smaller. Yet one is told at the Labour Exchange that one must look for a ship."[6]

The shipbuilding and repair industry on Merseyside was devastated by the slump. Even in the comparatively 'good' year of 1924 unemployment in the industry was 30%. By 1931, no less than 60% of shipyard workers were out of work.[7] Once a thriving industry in Birkenhead, Liverpool and Bootle, by 1932 there was only 11% of pre-war tonnage under construction. Boilermakers, riveters, turners and fitters – apprenticed dockside workers – became casuals, waiting each day at one of the fifty or sixty stands for work to come in. Taken on by the job, work could last just a few hours or maybe as long as a month. Most jobs lasted less than a week. Thousands of these workers were by 1932 living in appalling poverty.[8]

Untouched by Human Hand

The depression was not only reflected by job losses in the traditional industries. Local manufacturing industries, always overshadowed by the dominance of the port and few in number, had now entered a period of restructuring and rationalisation. Indeed, as we shall see in Chapter 8, the rationalisation programme of the thirties had a critical and irreversible impact on the way in which those people with jobs experienced the crisis. Even in the 'new' industries, expanding in terms of output and trade, such as the manufacture of artificial fibres, there was a net decline in the number of jobs available locally, and in 1932 about 14% of workers in the industry were out of work.[9] New machinery was increasingly replacing people. Those remaining found work was more intense and often more monotonous. People worked harder and faster, yet many found their wages cut.

Even established manufacturing industries on Merseyside, such as the food, drink and tobacco processing sectors, previously labour intensive at every stage of production, were now being 'streamlined'. Apprenticed cigarette makers became machine minders, bakers were replaced by giant dough mixers, bottles trawled around factories to be filled, labelled and packed by machinery. The advertisers' message, 'untouched by human hand', left middle class consumers to sleep soundly in their beds. Workers joined the long queue of the obsolete. Their skills, acquired over years, were no longer required.

Photo 4: Tobacco workers in Liverpool. Note the higher paid work like cutting and spinning is done by men, while lower paid work like cigarmaking and sorting is reserved for women. All suffered the effects of mechanisation and rationalism in the thirties.

Even the electrical engineering industry, particularly the manufacture of wirelesses and telephone equipment, was in difficulty by 1932. Thus, although the numbers employed in this 'industry of the future' had been steadily growing since the First World War, by 1932 one out of four of them were unemployed, and in the summer months at least 50% of those with jobs were laid off. Like so many local industries, work was seasonal and casual.[10]

For most of the unemployed chance became more important than experience for getting a job. Whenever the possibility arose of earning a few bob word quickly spread. The stand system, once the hallmark of the docks, now became the practice for all kinds of local work. You learned to be in the right place at the right time. As Billy Regan remembers,

"One thing that my father used to look forward to in the wintertime was the snow to come down. Because you could go and get employed by the corporation snow shifting and it was a big asset, you know...He'd be looking through the window and he'd say, 'Send it down JC'. And he used to go down to Vine Street, on the stand, and they'd pick so many hundred men on."[11]

No Future: Young and on the Dole

The scale of unemployment on Merseyside and its crushing impact on workers in the traditional industries combine to give an impression of uniformity amongst the unemployed. But whilst life on the dole created many shared experiences, particularly poverty, malnutrition and ill health, as the thirties progressed there also developed distinct divisions *within* the unemployed which were to have a political significance recognised by many at the time.

In this respect age played a crucial role. The issue of a generation of unemployed and 'unemployable' young people is familiar enough today but it is not entirely new. For example, a government committee, set up in the late twenties, expressed the following view:

"The disintegrating effect, moral and physical of juvenile unemployment is incalculable...We doubt whether sufficient attention has been given to the fate of the boys and girls who live in areas where the staple industries are especially depressed and where the atmosphere is charged with disillusionment and discouragement. In some districts, where employment is a comparative luxury, to allow girls and boys from fourteen to eighteen to roam the streets should be unthinkable. The unemployed boy of today is the unemployable man of tomorrow is a saying which we are satisfied is often only too true."[12]

At all times there is a value placed on experience and skill which almost invariably disadvantages the young. On the other hand, the cheapness of young labour is an attraction few industrialists could ignore. On Merseyside, however, the casual nature of the majority of industries created a very specific method of recruitment which almost always operated against the young. On the docks for example, even before the worst years of the depression, there existed a massive surplus of registered dockers. Having a docker's tally was never a guarantee of regular work and what became increasingly important was familiarity with the foreman. As a new face on the stand you were far less likely to be chosen than the person next to you who had been there twice a day for the last ten years or more. He was known and consequently he would be more likely to get the job. It is not surprising then, that in 1932 only 56% of men in their twenties in Liverpool were in regular employment, compared with 75% of those in their forties.[13]

Whilst the situation was marginally better for those aged between sixteen and twenty-one it was anything but good. Many girls and boys under sixteen could find work as messengers, delivery workers, in clerical jobs, making tea and sweeping floors. Although the wages for such work were abysmally low they were normally crucial to a family's income. But around the age of sixteen, the exact age varying from trade to trade, 'children' became 'adults', eligible for an adult job and an adult wage. They were sacked and replaced by the next group of school leavers. There was no automatic transfer from the tea room to the clerk's desk, or from messenger to postman.[14] And by sixteen it was too late to register as an apprentice. The young joined the thousands of unemployed who were trained and experienced in an unequal contest for scarce work. In any case, apprenticeships were hard to come by on Merseyside. There were relatively few local industries which required large numbers of time served workers, and most families simply couldn't afford to support a child learning a trade. As Jim Mottram, a railway worker, remembers,

"In those days on the railways, they were taking boys on at fourteen or fifteen and sacking them at twenty. And then they would replace them with younger staff. They were virtually running the railways on junior porters."[15]

By 1933, youth unemployment had become recognised as a serious problem locally and a special Committee of Enquiry was set up in Liverpool to examine the nature and extent of unemployment amongst fourteen to twenty year olds.[16] By the end of October 1934, there were 13,000 unemployed young people in Liverpool and with the sharp increase in the number of births which had taken place in the early twenties, the number was destined to rise until the Second World War found employment for all. The committee's report expressed its findings in terms which are frighteningly reminiscent of similar reports today.

"Many of the young unemployed have been without work for several years. Some have never worked since leaving school. Others have had no more than casual or intermittent employment, while not a few, after two or three years in fairly regular but definitely unprogressive employment, have been thrown out of their employment to make room for younger workers and have found it impossible to be absorbed in industry. The best years of their lives have thus, in more cases than it is possible to enumerate, been wasted altogether, and they have reached, or are rapidly reaching, an age beyond which the opportunities of acquiring skill in industry do not exist for them. For several years past this state of affairs has been a marked feature in the industrial life of Liverpool, and it would be impossible to estimate the loss that the City has suffered by its inability to utilise the surplus labour."[17]

No Dignity: Unemployed Women

Just as age divided the unemployed, so women found their experience of unemployment often quite different from that of men. Unemployment amongst men was a massive and conspicuous problem, a spectacle played out on the streets daily which no one could ignore. It was different for women, as for many reasons their unemployment was less obvious, but nonetheless just as real.

To a large extent the difficulty for women was that there were only a few large companies locally with a tradition of employing women workers. There was nothing to compare with the textile industry in the rest of Lancashire, where women were an accepted and significant section of the labour force. Of course this was not a situation unique to Merseyside. But there was something special about Merseyside in that the manufacturing sector was particularly small. And, of course, the predominant service industry – transport – was almost exclusively male. This forced the majority of women seeking to earn a living into the personal service sector, a grand title which meant for many women the hated job of domestic servant. Consequently, domestic service became a 'boom' area. but the poor conditions and wages of the domestic servant meant that this boom offered few benefits to women. Indeed, the boom was a direct consequence of the low pay of this type of work and the extent of unemployment among women.

Private domestic service made women the lonely slaves of the rich, almost completely cut off from friends, relatives and the outside world. As a Liverpool woman testified:

> "... first of all one is half a slave. The mistress thinks everything about one's life is her concern too. Because she is mistress one never has the chance to tell her she should mind her own business ... One is never free. Factory girls have certain working hours and then they are free. We have to work all day and there is never an end to it ... You can't bring a friend in even for a cup of tea ... Do you think it is pleasant to spend one's life with people who make one feel inferior to them? The loneliness is another factor, for sometimes it is days before you can speak to somebody who understands you."[18]

Even daily domestic work and office and factory cleaning involved little contact with other workers. Working in small groups, and often at night or in the early hours, this labour went almost unnoticed, and the social isolation presented such enormous problems of organisation that the women remained virtually without trade unions and subject to the poorest pay and worst working conditions in the area.

It is impossible to accurately assess the number of women involved in the service industry since much of the work was casual.[19] But between 1921 and 1931 the number of women officially recorded as working in the personal service sector in Liverpool rose from 31,000 to 38,000.[20] As male and female unemployment rose in the thirties, so more and more women sought domestic work as the only option. The surplus of workers created in the industry kept wages extremely low and prevented many older and less fit women from ever finding work again in their lifetimes once they became unemployed.[21] There is no doubt also that increasing numbers of married women were forced to find work on the fringes of the industry, taking in washing and ironing in order to make ends meet or to provide the only income in a family of unemployed workers. One man told us how his mother would walk from Edge Hill to Mossley Hill at the beginning of the week, collect some washing from a large house there, pawn it later in the day, take it out of pawn on Thursday, wash it on Friday and walk back to Mossley Hill on Saturday morning. Such ingenuity had little reward in a precarious industry.[22] Most of the work was not covered by the Insurance Scheme which meant that once unemployed the woman had no claim to unemployment benefit. Indeed, in

1932 only one half of working women on Merseyside were in insurable employment. Almost invisible as workers, when unemployed they simply disappeared from public record and concern.

Many Merseyside women were forced into the indignities of domestic work by changes taking place in other sectors of the economy. This was a period when women's claim to certain occupations was challenged; losses which in many cases women never regained. Perhaps most far-reaching in its subsequent implications was women's elimination from specific apprenticed jobs, particularly in the clothing, printing and tobacco industries. New machinery and processes introduced in the thirties often disadvantaged women workers, either in replacing their skill with machinery or with men, whose stronger trade unions were better able to claim for their members the diminishing areas of skilled work. Thus, for example, the introduction of mass-produced ready-made clothing in the thirties saw women increasingly relegated from skilled dressmakers to poorly paid machinist, whilst men, with the support of their unions, became concentrated in the design, cutting and finishing processes, all of which were apprenticed skills with higher pay, better working conditions and, most important, greater security.[23]

The vast majority of women factory workers on Merseyside were without an officially recognised trade, despite their skills. Many of these women found their occupations 'rationalised' in the thirties. Packing, labelling, bottle washing and a hundred and one other jobs were being transformed from hand to machine operations; a process which was continually cutting back areas where women had previously found work, however casual.

One ray of hope existed in the retail trade with the arrival of large chain stores in the town centres. For young single women work as a shop assistant offered a real alternative to domestic work but there were problems here too. In the first place, small local shops found they were unable to compete with the big stores in town and many were forced to close. The effects of this were felt particularly by married women, many of whom could work close to home, but were unable to take a job in town and leave their families for nine or ten hours a day. But the chain stores also depended on a supply of part-time labour to cover busy periods, especially during sales and weekends. In the New Year of 1933, for example, one large store in Liverpool took on 500 workers for the

January sales.[24] So despite increasing numbers of women being drawn into the trade, a considerable number were only casual workers.[25]

The already narrow and unattractive range of employment opportunities for women locally was worsened by the effects of the marriage bar, which operated in most industries except domestic service. Women were expected to leave their jobs on marriage. The majority had no choice. In 1932 therefore, only 10% of married women on Merseyside had insurable waged work.[26] Those married women relegated to the home also felt the effects of unemployment indirectly, as wives and mothers. They were expected to manage the meagre incomes of a family of unemployed workers. Many women simply did without in order to feed and clothe husbands and children, suffering all the anxiety of seeing those they loved and cared for thrown on the scrap heap.

No Rights: Black People and Unemployment

Liverpool and slavery are old friends. The shipowners and financiers of the port amassed their initial fortunes in the transportation of black people from Africa to the Caribbean Islands and the southern United States of America. Some were also brought to England as slaves but most worked on the sugar and tobacco plantations of the New World. The produce was shipped back to Liverpool for processing and sale. Traditionally, the sugar refineries and tobacco factories provided one of the few areas of shore-based employment. How ironic then that in the thirties black Liverpudlians were barred from many jobs, but especially " ... well, the tobacco factories – they didn't employ blacks there and the likes of Dunlops didn't employ blacks, or Tate and Lyles as well".[27] Black people were used and abused according to the dictates of profit and the practice was justified by the racism of British society.

Black settlement in Liverpool has a long history, going back to the days of slavery. In the later years of the last century, shipping lines on the West African run began to employ black firemen and trimmers beneath deck as wage labourers. And when, in 1911, the Seamen's Union gained recognition from the shipowners, part of the deal was that black seafarers would be paid much lower wages than white seafarers. By the thirties Liverpool was

"the only port in the country where the West African fireman are paid less than the white. In all other ports they are paid the same wages and belong to the union."[28]

Seafarers were recruited in West Africa but frequently they were paid off in Liverpool. As British passport holders they had, theoretically, free access to residence and employment in Britain. During the 1914-18 war, many black seamen were discharged in Liverpool when their boats were requisitioned by the Navy. They then sought and gained work here. But in the demobilisation which followed the signing of the Armistice in November 1918, the rights of black workers to live and work in Liverpool came under attack. In 1919, the *Liverpool Courier* estimated that 120 black workers had been dismissed from employment because white workers had refused to work with them. Ironically, in the wave of post-war labour 'militancy' white workers recreated discrimination. And a wider attack was launched on the right to reside in the city. Between 31st May and 10th June, a series of riots and attacks were made upon black people and black meeting places. One man, Charles Wooton, was drowned in the docks trying to escape from a mob of whites. Numerous others, over 700, were interviewed by the police, supposedly 'for their own good'. After discussions between the Lord Mayor, the Chief Constable, the Home Office and the Board of Trade, an unspecified number of black people were deported. The problem was defined, by employers, the state and the white working class, as the presence of black people.

But the state required a more systematic device to bar black people from the country. In 1925, the Coloured Alien Seamen's Order was passed in Parliament,

"one purpose of which was to check the influx of coloured alien seamen to this country".[29]

This Act required all black seamen resident in the country to register with the police and to carry a certificate bearing their photograph and thumbprint. In Liverpool, the order was extended. The Elder Dempster and John Holt shipping companies were granted exemption as they 'took responsibility for controlling their men while in port', and would deport them if no longer required. All the black seamen were, therefore, contract labourers with no rights.

As has been seen, opportunities for shore-based work were few and far between in the twenties and thirties; for black people they were even more limited. The League Against Imperialism reported in 1931 that the only firm which still employed black people in Liverpool was Bibby's –

and at the same wages as white workers. Ironically, it was strongly rumoured that Bibby's didn't employ Irish workers at the time. According to the *Daily Worker* one question black workers wanted answering was:

"Why is it that there are now hardly any firms in Liverpool and District where they can get employment on land? As soon as a manager or foreman sees them they are told that there is no place for coloured labour. Before and even during the war they used to be freely employed."[30]

A more systematic survey, carried out in 1930, found that out of 219 firms approached to take on young black people, only one responded by giving a trial. Additionally, out of 100 institutions or houses employing domestic labour, only four were willing to give a trial to a black woman. The report was forced to admit that this

"indicate(s) a general unwillingness on the part of employers to engage coloured labour."[31]

There clearly existed, then, a massive institutional discrimination against black people. They were forced to remain in the stokeholds, or, in the case of women, in sectors of the service industry like cafes, or in small tailoring back rooms.[32] In other words, black people in Liverpool were forced to work in those sectors of the economy where white workers were unwilling to work.

How extensive was unemployment amongst the black community in Liverpool in the thirties? In 1939, the University published a report on the economic condition of 'coloured families' in the city. 225 households were visited, 206 of these having adult men within the family. Nearly three-quarters of these men – 149 – were unemployed, the "great bulk" of them being classified as firemen or greasers on board ship. Throughout the thirties, oil was replacing coal as the motive power on board ship, which was one reason for the high level of unemployment amongst firemen. But the unemployment rate of 75% for black men was over twice as high as the *Social Survey of Merseyside* found, in 1931, amongst firemen as a whole. Shipping companies were obviously responding to the demands of the racist lobby to discriminate against black people in one of the major areas of employment that was open to them.

The 1939 survey went on to show that while over half of the black families were living on, or just under (a very meagre) poverty line, less than one-third of a sample of white families were living in 'poverty'.[32] It was hardly surprising that poverty was much more extensive amongst black families, given the higher rate of unemployment, but it was also due to the higher rents which black people were forced to pay. On average, black families paid 4s more a week in rent than white families. The report hesitantly concluded that

"the rent charged to coloured families may be a not unimportant factor in their depressed condition of life."[33]

As we shall show in Chapter 4, corporation housing rents were more expensive than those in privately rented housing. But this was not why black people were paying 40% more in rent than white people in the South End of Liverpool. "To be truthful, nearly all the black people had their houses from the landlord. Round our way the only corporation housing was Caryl Gardens and there were no blacks in there."[34] As one woman remembers, council housing was not let to black Liverpudlians: "before the war you didn't dare show your face on the outskirts".

Black people built Liverpool's former glory, along with the Irish, but when they came to live in the city, discrimination was their lot. The shipping lines were happy when black people signed on for work in Africa and they could pay them one half of a white seafarer's wage. But when Africans made their claim to live in Liverpool and sign on for work at the full rate, they were threatened with deportation. Black people became the 'problem'. After a report by Mabel Fletcher on the 'colour problem' in Liverpool the *Daily Worker* commented:

"It is significant the 'colour problem' arises when the supply of cheap labour is threatened. Professor P.M. Roxby, in the introduction to the report draws attention to the social menace which the colour problem in Liverpool presents. In point of fact, the negro population of Liverpool is probably one half of what it was some years ago when there was no immediate economic urge to 'produce a report' on the colour problem. It is now understood that government assistance will be sought to give official sanction to the conclusions."[35]

But the report did have another effect. In 1930, eighty black people in Liverpool founded Liverpool Negro Association whose aims were to "develop unity of Negro workers to struggle against capitalist exploitation, for united action for negro liberation and to assist the industrial organisation of negro workers".[36] Sections of this association contributed to the formation of the Coloured Seamen's Union later in the decade. They were certainly going to defend their right to live and work in Britain.

What was the response of the labour movement? At the 1930 TUC Conference, a delegate from the National Union of Seamen moved the following resolution:

"This congress views with alarm the continued employment of alien and undesirable coloured seamen and calls upon the government to ... provide remedial action."[37]

The argument was that the 1925 Order was not being strictly enforced – unregistered seamen were 'frequently' being discovered after police raids on boarding houses. Laws which would prevent "this class of seamen overrunning the British Merchant Marine" were called for. White workers were to have the jobs; black seamen should be sent home or expelled from the country. The Labour Government, when approached by the TUC, agreed to tighten up the system. It is hardly surprising that black people in Liverpool could not turn to the labour movement to support them in their struggle.

Notes

1. *Liverpool Daily Post*, 6.4.1929.
2. D. Caradog Jones, *Social Survey of Merseyside* (Liverpool University Press, 1934) Vol II. pp. 366, 369. Estimate of unemployment for both insured and uninsured workers.
3. Ministry of Labour, *Employment Gazette*; Pilgrim Trust, *Men Without Work* (Cambridge, Cambridge University Press, 1938).
4. Interview with George Hughes, 23.9.1983.
5. Caradog Jones, p.327.
6. *Daily Worker*, 3.7.30.
7. Caradog Jones, p.105.
8. Caradog Jones, pp.109-120.
9. Caradog Jones, pp.263-264.
10. Caradog Jones, pp.255-256.
11. Merseyside Socialist Research Group. Interview with Billy Regan.
12. Malcolm Committee proposals on youth training, quoted in *Hansard*, 9.11.1927.
13. Caradog Jones, p.377.
14. See, for example, report in Liverpool Daily Post, 9.4.1929.
15. Merseyside Socialist Research Group. Interview with Jim Mottram, 1981.
16. Joint Enquiry Committee on Unemployment among Young Persons in Liverpool, *Report upon the Nature and Extent of Unemployment among Young Persons between 14 and 21 years of Age* (City of Liverpool, 1935).
17. Report of Joint Enquiry Committee, pp.6-7.
18. Pilgrim Trust, p.260

19. This assessment is made even more difficult as there was no census taken in 1941, preventing us from analysing changes during the nineteen-thirties.

20. *Census of Population*, 1921 and 1931.

21. See Pilgrim Trust pp.250-251.

22. MSRG, recorded interview.

23. M.L.M. Reid, "Unemployment among Insured Women on Merseyside 1923-32" (Unpublished thesis, University of Liverpool, 1934).

24. *Liverpool Daily Post*, 3.1.1933.

25. Reid p.18, p.34; Caradog Jones pp.197-214.

26. Reid, *passim*.

27. MSRG Interview with Cath Terry, 10.11.1983.

28. M.E.Fletcher, *Report of an Investigation into the Colour Problem in Liverpool and Other Ports* (Liverpool, 1930), p.48.

29. Fletcher, p.8.

30. *Daily Worker*, 20.2.1931.

31. Fletcher p.33

32. University of Liverpool, *The Economic Status of Coloured Families in the Port of Liverpool* (Liverpool, 1940).

33. Ibid p.19

34. Interview with Cath Terry, 10.11.1983.

35. *Daily Worker*, 5.8.1930.

36. *Daily Worker*, 5.8.1930.

37. Trades Union Congress, *Report*, 1930

3
THE HUNGRY THIRTIES: POVERTY, MALNUTRITION AND ILL HEALTH

There is no greater indictment of a capitalist system in crisis than its tendency to let people suffer and die because they have too little to eat, too few warm clothes, and only cold and insanitary houses to live in. But such was the quality of life for millions of people in Britain throughout the thirties. Good health, good food and good housing are the most basic of human needs, yet in this period many working class people were denied even this. Of course, some contemporaries then, and conservative historians now, point to health statistics to indicate a clear improvement in people's health from the end of the nineteenth century onwards. But health statistics conceal a great deal.[1] In terms of our specific concerns in this book, many of the unemployed on Merseyside suffered from poor health as a direct consequence of their low income. And there were other groups within the working class, especially women, who suffered chronic ill-health in this decade. Indeed, for many the thirties was experienced, literally, as a daily struggle to stay alive. The tragedy, of course, is that many people died as a direct consequence of poverty and hopelessly inadequate medical aid and social services. Others took their own lives, overwhelmed by the desperation which haunted them.

Poverty and Malnutrition
By any standard the working class of Liverpool were one of the poorest and least protected groups within the country.[2] Poverty resulted directly from the compound effects of an economy characterised by unemployment, irregular employment, and low wage levels. Households with many children to feed were particularly prone to severe poverty.[3] There was simply not enough money in many homes to buy a diet adequate to protect a person from poor health. And it was clearly recognised at the time that diet was a key factor in improving health. As a nutritionist stated, in 1934,

"Many of the commoner physical ailments and defects could be reduced or even eliminated by proper feeding. Indeed, it is probably no exaggeration to say that proper feeding of the population of this country would be as revolutionary in its effects on public health and physique as was the revolution of cleanliness and drainage in the last century."[4]

Just as Edwina Currie, a Tory minister, lectured 'northerners' on their poor diet in the nineteen-eighties, so there were no end of 'authorities' in the nineteen-thirties willing to suggest 'efficient' ways for working class families to budget. Measly incomes, people were told, could purchase sufficient calories to stay alive if people shopped and ate wisely. In 1933, the British Medical Association, issued a report estimating the minimum cost of a diet adequate to maintain a person's "health and working capacity".[5] Based on a list of food prices which were, in fact, lower than those which obtained in many parts of the country, the report suggested a minimum of 5/11d for the weekly food bill for an adult male, 4/11d for an adult woman and 2/8d for a young child. Absurdly low as these estimates were, as we shall see, the Ministry of Health put their estimates even lower – at $5/1^{1}/_{2}$d for an adult male. But as the experience of a widow and her four children living in Index Street, Liverpool indicates, for many there was no possibility of affording even these theoretical minimums.

"The total income of the family is 28s and their expenditure is rent 9s, coal 2s, light and gas cooking 2s, polish, soap, boot repairs 2s, burial club 9d, clothing club 2s 6d."[6] (Leaving less than 10s. for food.)

The *Social Survey of Merseyside*, carried out by Liverpool University between 1929 and 1932, in fact provided detailed information on what was actually spent on food during these years by working class households. Among the unemployed average family size was two adults and four children and the total spending on food was 16s 9d for those on unemployment benefit and 18s 2d for those on public assistance.[7] If we take the B.M.A.'s recommendations for a *minimum* diet and apply them to families of this size, we find they should have been spending 25s 11d a week on food, i.e. 55% and 43% more respectively than they could actually afford.

Women appear to have suffered disproportionately from the effects of malnutrition. Women, and particularly mothers, have traditionally borne the responsibility of caring within the family. It is a role expected, and at times demanded, of them. As a result many women put the needs of their children, husbands and parents before their own. In the nineteen-thirties this bore tragically on women's health since many women simply did without food in order to feed their families.

"Mrs. F. of Liverpool is a widow and has four children under eight to keep on total housekeeping money of £1 17s 0d. She pays 10s 6d rent. Her own diet is extremely poor, consisting of bread and margarine, stew sometimes at dinner, no supper and never eggs, fish or vegetables. She suffers from anaemia and she says it is due to worry and under nourishment. But the Health Visitor says 'the children look well-fed and one cannot help believing that Mrs. F. is starving herself unnecessarily'."[8]

An insensitive comment from a doubtless well-fed health visitor.

Self-denial of this nature had particularly acute effects during pregnancy when a good diet was essential to the health of the woman and her baby. This was clearly recognised in the 1932 report of the Minister of Health, where it was argued

"After all, sound nutrition in a pregnant woman is obviously the only way of sustaining her health and strength and that of her forthcoming child. She should become accustomed to a diet which includes ample milk – two pints a day – cheese, butter, eggs, fish, liver, fruit and fresh vegetables, which will supply her body with the essential elements, salts and vitamins."[9]

But if we take the B.M.A.'s suggestion of 4/11d per week as the minimum expenditure on food for an adult woman, with milk at the time priced at $3^1/_2$d a pint, a woman would have spent all but 10d of her weekly allowance just buying the two pints of milk for herself each day. In fact working class families in Liverpool spent only between 5d and 1s per head a week on milk. And for the poorest families, particularly those on benefit, fresh milk would be beyond their reach – "conny onny" (condensed milk) would have to do.

It has to be said, also, that there is little joy in a life determined by a struggle to make ends meet and make do. The standards of the 'poverty line' estimators left no room for even the smallest of treats which can make life a little more bearable. As George Orwell observed in *The Road to Wigan Pier*,

"The ordinary human being would sooner starve than live on brown bread and raw carrots. And the peculiar evil is this, that the less money you have, the less inclined you feel to spend it on wholesome food ... When you are unemployed, which is to say when you are underfed, harassed, bored and miserable, you don't want to eat dull, wholesome food. You want something a little bit 'tasty' ... Unemployment is an endless misery that has got to be constantly palliated."[10]

People's Health

"One thing which will remain in the memory of anyone going around among the Liverpool unemployed will be the appalling housing conditions. [There was] ... an almost unending series of houses falling to pieces, long ago condemned as unfit for human habitation ..."

So commented the Pilgrim Trust report of 1936. A typical case in Liverpool was the situation of,

"the general labourer of 33, living with wife and four children (a daughter of six at school, another daughter crippled, a daughter of two and a son just born) in two rooms, small dark and damp, with the plaster decayed, nowhere to wash, gas used all day at a cost of 2s 6d a week, because there is no daylight – a necessity which substantially increases the gap between their net income of less than 34s and the 38s or so required by the 'poverty line' standard."[11]

Slum housing, as we shall see in Chapter Four, was a major social problem on Merseyside and people's health inevitably suffered in such conditions. The clearest indicators of the relationship between bad housing and poor health were the epidemics which swept dockside areas. Although some of the most horrific infectious diseases of the previous century, like cholera and typhoid, were by this time under control, in 1928 there was an outbreak of smallpox in Ellesmere Port which spread to Liverpool in 1929.[12] Even typhoid reappeared in Widnes in 1927,[13] and in 1929 a major influenza epidemic reached Britain from the United States of America. It was particularly severe in industrial areas, and despite the fact that Liverpool was not as badly hit as elsewhere, 400 people in the city died. It was focused in the city centre where it combined with an epidemic of measles which swept through local schools, closing many of them. In one week in January, 140 people died from respiratory diseases and Walton Poor Law Hospital alone admitted 180 patients suffering from 'flu. Such was the crisis in the hospital that forty-seven members of staff contracted the illness and the strain on resources was such that many patients had to be treated in corridors. By the end of May there had been 6000 cases of measles reported in the city. 770 of these cases were admitted to hospitals and 283 died.[14]

Thus although the death rate from some infectious diseases did decline throughout the thirties in Liverpool, measles, whooping cough, diptheria and influenza remained major killers.

TABLE ONE
AVERAGE DEATHS PER YEAR FROM:

	Measles/German measles	Diptheria	Influenza	Whooping Cough
1926-30	268	135	198	171
1931-35	273	177	215	133

Source: *Annual Reports of Medical Officer of Health, Liverpool 1926-1935.*

Harry Livermore, who moved from Newcastle to Liverpool in the thirties remembers his first months here.

"I was so shocked by the conditions that existed here ... You saw children in bare feet – that was quite common in the poorer districts. You saw women in filthy weather without coats, just simply a shawl wrapped around them ... the courts around St. Anne's, Crispin Street, were really cul-de-sacs. About 500 families living in these courts with one outside loo ... and when that got stopped up the health hazards were enormous. If you went round there once, well, it was a shattering experience."[15]

Conditions such as these inevitably encouraged the spread of infectious diseases. Indeed, in some inner city areas the new public health schemes dealing with sewage, refuse disposal and water supply had very little effect, as the following account indicates.

"In Mount Vernon Terrace, off Mount Vernon Green, there are eleven three-bedroomed houses. The entrance to the terrace is three to four feet wide. Children have suffered from pneumonia in the last twelve months. Only two of the 32 adults in the street are in employment. One pump supplies water and there are two bins in which they put all their rubbish. These bins are situated at the entrance to the terrace. There are two W.C's for the use of eleven houses."[16]

In inner city areas, like St. Anne's ward, poor housing and sanitation meant that the death rate was considerably higher than in the more prosperous areas of the city. For instance, in the Baptist Street area the death rate between 1921 and 1928 was 22.5 per 1000 compared with a rate of 13 per 1000 for the city as a whole. Similarly, the infant mortality rate for the area was 158.86 per 1000 births over the same period, compared with a figure of 100.2 per 1000 for the city as a whole.[17]

Again, across the river in the Moreton area of Wallasey the local Medical Officer of Health was quoted as follows:

"The area of 28 acres contained roughly 630 houses and other erections – 22 to the acre as against 10 to 12 in modern housing schemes. The majority of the houses were no bigger than a fair sized room and in this very restricted space many families lived and slept. At any moment an epidemic might arise.[18]

He added that the whole site was under water in wet weather, that there was an absence of drainage and that the houses drained directly into cess pools.

What these housing conditions meant for the health of individual families can be seen starkly in this example of a family living in the Crosshall Street area.

"In one room less than twelve feet square we found a man and his wife and four children. One of the children was suffering from TB. The father, who had fought four years in the war, also had TB. There was only one bed for six people, no place to do the washing but a small tub, a miserable table in the centre of the room and one broken chair."[19]

Of course young children were particularly prone to poor health and death as a result of poor and insanitary housing. For example, in the Exchange ward near Liverpool city centre, 350 children under the age of two died from diarrhoea and enteritis in 1927. The Medical Officer of Health termed it an epidemic of 'summer diarrhoea' caused by insanitary conditions. He added that breastfeeding was a protection and that 'no child should be weaned, if possible, between July and October'. The view of an 'expert' who no doubt had never himself had to breastfeed. Yet again mothers were being asked to make the extra sacrifice.[20]

Depression

It was not only people's physical health which suffered under the strain of poverty and unemployment. Depression and mental illness ruined the lives of many of the unemployed. Throughout the twenties and thirties there was a constant stream of reports of suicides in the local press. Often these suicides were linked directly to poverty and unemployment.

For instance, Charles Hughes, aged fifty-two, a dock labourer, threw himself under a lorry. He had worked the previous season in the Isle of Man "and having failed on his return to get work at the docks was depressed". On the same day John Firman, a shipyard worker, hung himself. "He was depressed by the fear of losing his job". Alfred Court, aged thirty-four, from Waterloo, gassed himself. He had been a soldier until

1921, and for the following seven years had only been able to get occasional casual employment. His mother said "the fact that he was out of work preyed on his mind and he was depressed". William Bagwell, aged sixty-two, a dock labourer, committed suicide. His daughter stated that "her father had been out of work for four years and had been depressed for the last two years". Samuel Humphrey, aged sixty-five, of Kensington, hung himself from the banister in his home. "He had been unemployed for eighteen months and had suffered from depression owing to his inability to find work". A woman from Kirkdale, aged twenty-three, attempted to poison herself. It was her third attempted suicide. At her trial she stated that "she lived with her brother, 15/3d was coming in every week and their rent alone was 10/- per week. She was worried and depressed." James Gordon, aged forty-two, from the Dingle, a father of six children, gassed himself. He had been unemployed for two and a half years and none of his five children still living at home was working. His wife said "her husband was worried that because there was only the dole coming in they'd be short for Christmas". Catherine McKenzie, aged twenty-four, from Everton, hung herself from the banister. Her husband had been out of work for eighteen months and she had been depressed for nine months after the birth of their youngest child. Her husband stated "the only worry was unemployment".[21]

A list of tragedy and despair.

Working Conditions and Illness

In November 1929, eleven workers were killed by a huge explosion at Bibby's Oil Seed Milling factory on the Dock Road. The tragedy of these deaths inevitably hit the headlines, but in fact industrial accidents resulting in death and serious injury occurred on an almost daily basis in the inter-war years. To lose one's life whilst creating profits and wealth for the ship and factory owners was the ultimate sacrifice of working class people. And the scramble for increased production and fatter profits pursued in the thirties meant many workers made this sacrifice. The speed up and intensification of work witnessed in the thirties, and which we document in Chapter 8, invariably led to scant regard for the safety and health of workers. In 1932 on Merseyside there were 3,149 industrial accidents reported to the Factory Inspectorate. Over the next four years there was a sharp rise in industrial accidents, the figure for 1935 being 5,021. A further sharp increase in the following years meant that by 1939 there were 6,882 cases recorded. In seven years, then, industrial accidents on Merseyside had more than doubled.[22] Whilst this increase could partly be accounted for by an increase in the numbers of employed workers, such a dramatic rise indicates the ruthless effects of speed up and rationalisation. Indeed the speed up of work caused anxiety and stress to many workers and hanging over them all was the constant worry that the sack would come if not today, then tomorrow, next week, next month ...

Many women in waged work on Merseyside suffered an exploitation at work far more intense than that of their husbands and fathers, since they tended to work in small workshops and in uninsured jobs, outside the supervision and control of the Factory Inspectorate. Even where conditions in an industry in which women worked were controlled by an Act of Parliament employers were able to flout the law as a result of the weaker union organisation of women. In 1928, Ellen Wilkinson raised a question in Parliament concerning the women who worked as sack makers and menders in the warehouses along the Dock Road in Liverpool. She asked the Home Secretary whether he was aware,

"that the terms and conditions of the Sacks (Cleaning and Repairing) Welfare Order, 1927 have not been given effect to in Liverpool, where a large number of women are employed under wretched conditions in old warehouses; that several employers are making no attempt to provide overalls, dining room accommodation etc for their workpeople."[23]

But by 1930 nothing had been done. Conditions in the warehouses remained reminiscent of those which had appalled nineteenth century reformers,

"... like dungeons, where girls and women are allowed the sum of 6d an hour for mending, stowing, loading and unloading heavy bundles of sacks. After a few hours at this the women become choked with grain and mineral dust and their clothing swarms with weevils and similar insects. Many of the girls fail to complete a day's work."[24]

Low wages, long hours of work and insanitary and unhealthy workplaces were the day to day reality for many women workers.

Women's Health
But many women were both waged workers and mothers, labourers outside the home as well as inside it. And in the thirties on Merseyside the double burden which women shouldered sapped their strength and vi-

tality and wrecked the health of many, for it was borne in a context of poor housing and insufficient income. As Marjorie Spring Rice reported on the information collected from 1,250 married working women by the Women's Health Enquiry Committee,

"It is the cumulative effect of years of ever increasing toil which even if it results in no definite disease (or in none that they can specify) crushes the vitality of so many working mothers and reduces them too often by the age of 40 or 50 to a grievous and irredeemable state of health."[25]

We must never forget the staggering toll in women's lives in the thirties caused by poverty and overwork. Many married women raising families were forced to work excessively long hours in order to make ends meet. They took in washing, ironing and sewing and often worked into the early hours, while children slept, in order to make a few extra shillings for the family purse. The pressure on women to keep their jobs led many to carry on working when they felt ill or were suffering from ailments such as anaemia or dysmenorrhea. Such ill-health was almost taken for granted.[26]

There was clear evidence at the time of this widespread suffering and sickness amongst married women. There was also official recognition

Photo 5: Pawning clothes to make ends meet – the strain on women caused by unemployment and poverty took a heavy toll on their health.

that this general level of ill health was exacerbated by childbirth. One estimate was that 10% of women in Britain were "more or less crippled by childbirth"[27] and reports from a variety of doctors and officials in Liverpool, Glasgow and Edinburgh confirmed that, 'more than 30% of women attending gynaecological departments were suffering from some form of maternal disablement.[28]

But this huge problem of suffering amongst women was considered beyond the scope of Government. As Sir George Newman, Chief Medical Officer of Health between 1919 and 1935, commented in response to demands for an enquiry into morbidity (sickness) amongst women,

"[it could] have but one ending, namely, the demonstration of a great mass of sickness and impairment attributable to childbirth, which would create a demand for organised treatment by the state ... childbirth has always been women's travail and always will be ... the broad fact remains, first, that childbirth is a heavy strain on the physique of any woman and the bodies of many must therefore be impaired; secondly, that there is in modern civilised nations an insufficiency of organised facilities for effective treatment."[29]

Governments committed to restricting public expenditure would never countenance the provision of appropriate facilities.

Mass unemployment clearly kept alive the ideology that "a woman's place was in the home". Women in the labour market were viewed as a potential threat – they might displace men in what were seen as 'male jobs'. Indeed, the whole tenor of the period effectively kept women on the fringes of the economy, in uninsured, poorly paid work. And within the home women not only bore the stress of managing meagre incomes but almost invariably had total responsibility for housework and childcare. The Women's Health Enquiry Committee revealed, in the poignant testimony of one woman, how disabling and depressing this experience could be.

"I believe myself that one of the biggest difficulties our mothers have is our husbands do not realise we ever need any leisure time. My life for many years consisted of being penned in a kitchen nine feet square, every fourteen months a baby, as I had five babies in five years at first, until, what with the struggle to live and no leisure, I used to feel I was just a machine, until I had my first breakdown. And as dark as it was and as hard as it was it gave me the freedom and the privilege of having hours of fresh air. And so I truly know that this is the the lot of many a poor mother. I know my third baby had rickets, but what could I do, I was expecting another little one and already had a baby three years of age

Photo 6: A group of "tired mothers" enjoy a brief rest from their every-day toil at a Rest Home in Allerton run by charity – but for most working class women there was no chance of this respite.

and one two years. So many of our men think we should not go out until the children are grown up. We do not want to be neglecting the home but we do feel we would like to have a little look around the shops, or if we go to the Clinic we can have just a few minutes ... It isn't that the men are unkind. It is the old idea we should always be at home."[30]

Birth Control and Abortion

It was in the twenties and thirties that various women's organisations and campaigning bodies began to put pressure on the Government to provide women with birth control and abortion facilities. It was well known at the time that women, faced with frequent pregnancies, resorted to abortion. Women had their own, often extremely dangerous, remedies for unwanted pregnancies. Others used illegal back street abortionists who rarely had sufficient medical knowledge to carry out a termination of pregnancy without endangering the life of the woman. In 1936 the British Medical Association estimated that between 16% and 20% of all pregnancies ended in abortion, and that of all deaths in childbirth one in six occurred at the time of abortion.[31]

Because abortion was illegal pregnant women became easy prey for the extortionate charges of the back street. In February 1935 a Doctor Siddall was jailed for five years at Liverpool Assizes having been found guilty of manslaughter. He had been charged with the murder of a twenty-eight year old woman who had died a few days after he aborted her. The woman died from haemorrhage and septic infection – common causes of death at the hands of an unskilled abortionist. The post-mortem revealed that "considerable and excessive force" had been used, and the court heard that the woman had paid £70 – a fee way beyond the reach of working class women.[32] Instead women attempted to abort themselves, using knitting and darning needles, crotchet hooks, scissors, pencils, disinfectants, dolly blue or alcohol, but often with the same tragic results.[33]

Evidence of the dangers of unskilled abortion was one of the bases on which women's organisations argued for the more widespread availability of birth control. But little headway was made in this period in convincing governments that birth control advice and facilities were services which should properly be provided by the state. The only move, made in 1930, was to agree to provide birth control information to women whose health it was considered would be seriously damaged by further pregnancy. As Jane Lewis comments, "women had to be very sick to qualify".[34] Instead women had to depend for birth control advice on voluntary organisations, such as the one established in Liverpool in 1925. However, advice from such organisations reached few working class women in the face of medical, religious and political opposition. In Liverpool Bessie Braddock's attempts to improve the quality of the birth control services available to local women met with the full force of Catholic opposition within the Labour Party. In 1936, she was rebuked by the Labour Group for an attack she made on Councillor Bevins of Abercromby Ward whom she accused of having, "voted against the best interests of working class mothers on the birth control issue".[35]

Maternal Mortality

Most damaging to the state's position on the question of health was the evidence that maternal mortality had risen by 25% in England and Wales between 1920 and 1936. A Ministry of Health enquiry was established to examine the problem, but in its report it rejected any relationship between, on the one hand, poor diet and poor housing and, on the other, death during childbirth.[36] Again, the emphasis was placed on women using neighbourhood maternal welfare services. There was also a growing tendency throughout the thirties for childbirth to take place in hospital. Between 1927 and 1937 the proportion of births in hospital rose from 17% to 35% of all births and, according to an obstetric textbook of the time, in order to make childbirth safe every labour had to be treated as a "major surgical procedure".[37]

This transition was extremely rapid in Liverpool, where by 1935, nearly half of all births took place in institutions.[38] Indeed, although it was only two thirds built at the end of 1927, the Oxford Street Maternity Hospital in Liverpool had already dealt with 1,200 women by the end of that year – a 50% increase on the 1923 figure. By 1929 the Poor Law Guardians had established maternity wards at Walton, Mill Road and Smithdown Road where at any one time seventy women could be accommodated in ten wards.[39]

Photo 7: The Minister of Health exchanges pleasantries with a pramful of children at the opening of a Maternity and Child Welfare Centre in Walton, 1937. Just behind him is Bessie Braddock, MP, who fought fiercely for the extension of facilities like this for women. Nevertheless, provision remained extremely poor throughout the thirties.

Whilst women clearly welcomed the provision of any services which improved the safety of childbirth, the issue was not clear cut. Both women's organisations and midwives stressed the beneficial effects which improvements in home-based maternity services would bring. Thus, for example, the President of the Liverpool and District Trained Midwives Association complained at their 1928 conference that public opinion had been swayed into thinking that hospital was the ideal situation for all confinements. She argued that, in fact, this was necessary only where complications or illness existed. What was at issue in this debate over the hospitalisation of childbirth was the competition between doctors and midwives to carve out for themselves a monopoly of expertise in the fields of obstetrics. Clearly the doctors won the day but the stress placed by midwives on the importance of a more 'homely' service was borne out by later research and experience. As Jane Lewis has argued, the hospitalisation of childbirth had little impact on the rate of women's death for the key to safe deliveries was the presence of a careful attendant.[40] What was lost in the debate and in subsequent practice was a consideration of the desires of individual women on where and how they wished the birth of their children to take place.

Cover Up

"There is at present no medical evidence of any general increase in the physical impairment, sickness or mortality as a result of the economic depression or unemployment."[41]

So stated Sir E. Hilton Young, Minister of Health, in 1933. But as the thirties progressed this official view of an increasingly fitter and healthier population, undamaged by the effects of unemployment, was challenged from all sides. For whilst the annual reports of Medical Officers from around the country consistently painted this picture of progress, there was growing criticism of such optimism from a variety of pressure groups concerned with health issues, such as the Women's Co-operative Guild, the State Medical Services Association (later the Socialist Health Association), the National Unemployed Workers Movement and even from health officials.

As we have seen, the health of people on Merseyside was anything but good. Indeed, if we take the infant mortality rate as an accepted indicator of general standards of health we find that in 1933 the rate for St. Helens was 116 per 1,000 live births, for Liverpool 98, whereas for Oxford it was 32. General statistics indicating improvements in health in fact concealed wide regional variations. Even within Liverpool itself the infant mortality rates remained consistently high throughout the inter-war years in inner city areas, whilst in more prosperous areas of the city the rate declined. Thus, in Abercromby Ward and Everton the rate remained around 25% above the city average between 1933 and 1939, whilst in areas such as West Derby and Wavertree it was about 25% below the average. Improvements in health standards were by no means matched by a narrowing of the gap between the classes; indeed in some respects the gulf widened in the nineteen-thirties compared with earlier in the century.[42] And as we have seen, class and locality were not the only factors governing a person's health; gender was also crucial here.

Charles Webster has convincingly demonstrated not only the extent of malnutrition and ill-health amongst the working class and the unemployed in particular, but also the way in which the state sought to cover up this massive problem which claimed the lives of so many. The word from Whitehall sent out to local Medical Officers was to be as cheerful as possible in reports on the health of local populations. Local Medical Officers who in fact drew the obvious links between economic crisis and mortality rates found themselves censured by the Ministry of Health. Frazer, the Medical Officer for Liverpool in the nineteen-thirties, took the government directive to report optimistically very seriously! So much so that even officials within the Ministry found his returns 'frankly incredible'. This is not surprising when we find that the rate of malnutrition in Bootle was recorded to be twelve times that of Liverpool! There were also technical problems in defining issues such as the extent of malnutrition since there existed no agreement on the scientific measurement and diagnosis of malnutrition. Thus reports were often arbitrary and subjective.

The attitude of successive governments to the health of the population in the thirties reveals the blatant cynicism with which political office is at times maintained. A genuine commitment to improving the health of working class people would have required a level of public expenditure which no government of the time was prepared to countenance. Rates of benefit were simply too low for men and women. Housing conditions on Merseyside encouraged the spread of deadly infectious diseases. Mothers were worn out by childbirth and worry. And no amount of re-writing of history can ever bring back those who took their lives in despair believing improvements would never come.

Notes
1. Charles Webster, 'Healthy or Hungry Thirties?', *History Workshop Journal*, Spring, 1982.
2. The Pilgrim Trust, *Men Without Work* (Cambridge, Cambridge University Press, 1938).
3. *Men Without Work*, p.97.
4. John Stevenson, *British Society 1914-45* (Harmondsworth, Penguin, 1984) p.206.
5. W. Hannington, *The Problem of the Distressed Areas* (Wakefield, E.P. Publishing, 1976), p.56-57.
6. *Daily Worker*, 27.7.1932.
7. D. Caradog Jones, *Social Survey of Merseyside* (Liverpool, Liverpool University Press, 1934) Volume 1, p.236.
8. Margery Spring Rice, *Working Class Wives: Their Health and Conditions* (Harmondsworth, Penguin, 1939), p.167.
9. Quoted in Hannington, *The Problem...*, p.55.
10. George Orwell, *The Road to Wigan Pier* (London, Secker and Warburg, 1973), p.96-97
11. Pilgrim Trust, pp.94-95
12. See Reports in *Liverpool Daily Post* 28.2.1928; 9.8.1928; 19.11.1928; 18.1.1929.
13. *Liverpool Daily Post* 21.7.27.
14. *Liverpool Daily Post*, 23/24.1.1929; 6.7.1929.
15. Merseyside Socialist Research Group. Interview with Harry Livermore.
16. Letter to *Daily Worker* from Liverpool tenant, 30.7.1932.
17. Ministry of Health Enquiry quoted in *Liverpool Daily Post*, 2.5.1928
18. *Liverpool Daily Post*, 27.7.1928.
19. *Liverpool Daily Post*, 2.10.29.
20. *Liverpool Daily Post*, 28.9.1928
21. See Reports in *Liverpool Daily Post*, 30.9.27; 15.6.28; 5.3.29; 12.10.29; 5.7.33; 28.12.33; 27.2.1935
22. Annual Reports of the Chief Inspector of Factories and Workshops, 1932-39.
23. *Hansard*, 5.6.1928.
24. *Daily Worker*, 7.3.1930.
25. Spring Rice, p.50.
26. Spring Rice, p.49.
27. Jane Lewis, "In Search of Real Equality: Women Between the Wars" in F. Gloversmith (ed.), *Class, Culture and Social Change*, (Brighton, Harvester, 1980), p.221.
28. Webster, p.122.
29. Lewis, pp.221-2.
30. Spring Rice, p.94.
31. Lewis, p.227.
32. *Liverpool Daily Post*, 5.2.1935, 9.2.1935.
33. *Report of the Inter-Departmental Committee on Abortion* (HMSO, London, 1939), p.41.
34. Lewis, p.229.
35. Liverpool Trades Council & Labour Party Minutes, 1936.
36. Ministry of Health, *Report of an Investigation into Maternal Mortality* (HMSO, April 1937), pp.278-9, 123-4.
37. Lewis, p.219.
38. *Liverpool Daily Post*, 4.1.1937.
39. *Liverpool Daily Post*, 12.2.1929.
40. J. Lewis, *The Politics of Motherhood: Child and Maternal Welfare in England 1900-1939*, (1980).
41. Quoted in Hannington, *The Problem...*, p.49.
42. Webster, p.116.

4
"BOLD AND IMAGINATIVE" ... BUT THE SLUMS REMAIN: LIVERPOOL'S HOUSING BETWEEN THE WARS

"The development of Merseyside, the tunnel, the ring road and the bold and imaginative housing schemes demonstrate the desire of Liverpool to implement constructive and imaginative planning. In addition, Liverpool seems to have a penchant for collecting famous cathedrals and one may presume from this that Liverpool has an ambition to build a new Jerusalem. I have therefore come to this city as one who respects and admires its great status as an outstanding example of the larger cities of the country."[1]

So said Herbert Morrison on a visit to Liverpool a couple of years after work had started on the new Catholic cathedral, so perhaps he can take credit for initiating the "cathedral to spare" jibe. Indeed, as the Metropolitan cathedral was intended to be second in size only to St. Peter's in Rome, it was a construction to marvel at. But Morrison's main interest was directed towards the housing of the humble, rather than with the houses of God.

Liverpool Corporation built around 39,000 houses and flats between the wars, and by 1939 about one-fifth of Liverpool families lived in council dwellings built in the previous twenty years. Morrison, the emerging Labour boss of the London County Council, was impressed by the scale of this achievement; more so because it was supervised and developed by a Tory council. How can this be explained? Can Toryism have a progressive face?

Insurance Against Bolshevism – The nineteen-twenties
In looking at public sector housing between the wars a number of points have to be borne in mind. The state had only recently been encouraged to undertake housing provision. Even up to 1914, it was assumed that private builders would put up houses for the working class. After 1918 the state's intervention, by granting subsidies to local authorities for house construction, was primarily a political response to growing labour and socialist militancy. Union organisation, socialist politics, sympathy with the Soviet Union and Sinn Fein all had to be combated. Lloyd George took out his "insurance against Bolshevism" with the Addison

Act which thrust local authorities into house building. The Act did not make house building compulsory – it merely allowed local authorities some financial support should they wish to develop council housing. But throughout the twenties housing provision changed as the balance of class forces changed.

The Chamberlain Act passed by the Tory government in 1923 restricted subsidies for public housing and, hardly surprisingly for the Tory Party, gave subsidies straight to the private builders. The following year the first Labour Government put through one of its few memorable pieces of legislation – the Wheatley Act – which reallocated substantial subsidies to local councils. Now there were two parallel schemes, for the public and private sectors. But after the defeat of the General Strike in 1926 and the deflationary policies that accompanied the return to the gold standard, all public expenditure was cut. Housing subsidies were slashed, public housing programmes collapsed and new starts virtually ceased by 1930. Thus the decade after the First World War saw three major phases of state policy towards public sector housing – its initial establishment, the extension under Labour, and the drastic cutbacks at the end of the decade.

From Green Fields to Slum Clearance – The Nineteen-thirties

Housing expenditure was an easy target for the Government of the day to attack – it was a relatively new area of social provision and cuts weren't immediately noticeable. Despite considerable administrative problems, councils had used the novel Housing Acts quite extensively. In Liverpool, Norris Green, Clubmoor, Dovecot and Fazakerley estates were all built under the Wheatley Act. The council built 6,000 houses in 1927 alone. Unfortunately, these achievements were often considered by the authorities to have "solved" Liverpool's housing problems. Supporting evidence was frequently provided in local reports for this astounding assumption, usually from the Medical Officers of Health. Housing reports, however, were no more "objective" than those relating to health referred to in the previous chapter. In many cases they had been doctored and represented the most crude public relations exercise, aimed at absolving central Government from any responsibility for slum conditions. How else can we explain the Bootle M.O.H.'s testimony at a housing enquiry in 1934 that there were "no slums in Bootle"? Maybe there was another Bootle then?

The election of the second Labour Government in 1929 altered the direction of state housing policy. It passed legislation, known as the Greenwood Act, aimed at slum clearance and rehousing. In the twenties, council housing had been the preserve of the regularly employed working class. Labour suggested that the focus should change and now be directed at the rehousing of slum dwellers of the inner city. For houses built under the new Act were to be of a lower standard and would be heavily subsidised from central Government, and so cheaper for local authorities. In effect, however, in some eyes this created two classes of council tenant – the barely deserving and the clearly undeserving!

Again, Liverpool utilised the provisions in the Act but by 1933 the new National Government had made slum clearance the *only* grounds for local authority involvement in house building. Private enterprise, it was forcefully argued, would cater for "general needs". It is doubtful if the National Government ever believed their own propaganda. What is clear is that the expanding building industry totally failed to build enough homes for rent for working people. By 1939 the shortage of homes in Liverpool was as severe as it had been twenty years beforehand.

Gardens, Hedges and Trees on 'Parish Green'
In the twenties when the first 'Addison' houses were built, the council found there was an immediate demand for rented council houses. Most of them were built in leafy suburbs, previously green fields – 2,000 at Larkhill, 800 on Edge Lane Drive and 1,000 at Springwood near Allerton. These were the cream of Liverpool's council housing ... the first ones to be sold off in the nineteen-eighties. The houses were built to generous specifications on a garden-suburb model. Very low population densities prevailed on the estates with wide grass verges, trees and large gardens. Housing that the war had been fought for, as Lloyd George was so fond of saying! Jim Mottram's family moved to Springwood soon after it was completed:

"Springwood wasn't a big estate. A very nice estate, a very select estate. We were lucky I suppose. Although homes were easy to get in those days, the Echo had page after page of adverts of houses to rent – 10 shillings, 17 shillings a week or whatever. But for us this was a steep increase from 7 shillings a week in a house which had only these four rooms, one cold tap, no hot water or bathroom, no electric light but one gas light in the kitchen and everywhere else was illuminated by candles. So fuel bills were very low indeed. As well as this was the cost of transport, because my sisters and the other members of the family had to use the trams, so this was a stiff increase in expenditure. But of course that's balanced against the fact that my father (a boilermaker) was in full employment and my sisters were also working."[2]

Clearly, Jim Mottram's family were better able than some to afford the higher rents on Springwood. For many tenants the move to the garden suburbs was fraught with difficulties. The major problem was money – the rent. Norris Green was nicknamed 'parish green' at the time, reflecting the number of residents who were on relief.

Many families found it impossible to make ends meet. Eleanor Rathbone reported on conditions in Norris Green in 1929, mainly to illustrate the need for a family allowance system. She recorded:

"Many children visibly suffering from malnutrition so severe as to produce boils, anaemia, colic etc.; badly broken boots, insufficient underclothing, hence bad attendance at school; many houses stripped almost bare of furniture, everything having been pawned or sold to pay the rent; many verminous houses (women say nothing left to buy soap); many tenants deeply in debt to the money lenders, endeavouring to pay several shillings a week interest in addition to high rents; fathers, sons and daughters engaged in, or in search of, work either obliged to walk several miles in or out of town on worn-out boots, or pay 4d a day in tram fares; general mood one of sullen anger, deep depression or apathetic resignation; general verdict summed up in one woman's remark – 'we've got a posh house but the children are clemming' (starving)."

She concluded:

"... our policy has done much for small families, especially of clerks and artisans etc., but almost nothing for unskilled labourers, especially those with large families."[3]

The secretary of the Tenants Defence League on the estate, set up to prevent evictions, wrote to the *Daily Worker*:

"The houses are brilliantly illuminated with electric light – that is when we have a bob to spare. We get $3^{1}/_{2}$d discount out of every shilling we put in the meter and oh!, what rejoicing when the collector calls ... if we haven't put too many washers in, in which case we are not at home."[4]

Average council house rents in Liverpool in the early nineteen-thirties were 14s a week, in contrast to an average private rent of 10s a week. It was also clear that additional expenditure, on top of the rent, made the 'sunshine houses' of the outer estates very expensive options. Larger houses had to be furnished. Hot running water was available but it had to be paid for, along with lighting, heating and even a spade for the garden and shears for the ubiquitous privet hedge. All additional expenses. Tram fares had to be allowed for – relatives and work were no longer 'just around the corner'. The few shops that existed on the new estates took advantage of their monopoly position to charge higher prices. Faced with all this many families were forced to moonlight back to the cheaper but overcrowded accommodation by the docks.

There was a constant problem over people's inability to afford council house rents right through the nineteen-thirties in Liverpool, and also a constant struggle over their level. In 1931 the Council received a petition from 10,000 tenants organised by the Liverpool Council of Corporation Tenants Associations, asking for a reduction. The levels had been fixed, they claimed, "when the country was booming", many tenants were now unemployed, others had suffered wage reductions and travelling costs were high. Rents were 'excessive' they petitioned.[5] There were reductions in response to such campaigning – for instance in 1934 rents were reduced by between 2d and 1/- per week – but this was little more than a gesture.[6] The problem persisted right up to August 1939, when tenants on the Longview estate were organising a rent strike over 'excessive' rents.[7]

Housing – The Bad ...

In October 1933, the *Liverpool Daily Post* carried the following report.

"Myriads of cockroaches swarmed from Midghall Street, off Vauxhall Road, climbed up the walls of the houses and entered through the windows, beneath the doors and any aperture they could find. The street is flanked on the west side by the walls of Bibby's seed crushing mill and to these thousands of insects clung, while a great mass crawled up the houses opposite for a distance of fity yards. The occupiers were kept from their beds during Saturday night and Sunday morning, trying to get rid of the pests. It is believed they came out of the sewers."[8]

The University Settlement provided another account in its report on *'Housing Conditions in Liverpool, 1931'*. It quoted one example of a single house occupied by six families.

"Family of five on ground floor. One room. Rent 4s. Husband unemployed. Rats as big as kittens reported. Family extremely anxious to move anywhere decent.

Young family of six in two rooms at back on ground floor. Income 55s a week. Rent 7s.

Sick man and wife in front room upstairs. Unemployed for a long period. They said rain water drained into the cellar from outside passage and caused bad smells.

Husband and wife in one upstairs room. Man unemployed. Rent 4s. Room in bad state of repair. Complaints re. dustbin.

Mother and two children in one back room. In receipt of parish relief. Rent 3s.

Widow in one room at the top. OAP. Rent 4s. Very bad state of repair of the room. She dreaded the pulling down of the house because she feared that she wouldn't be able to afford one of the new ones."[9]

Nineteen people in one house of seven rooms!

Similarly, a local priest found appalling conditions in his parish of Holy Cross. At a meeting in the church hall, Father Michael O'Ryan said,

"Down one side of Gerard Street, 790 people are living in 48 houses ... In twelve of these houses, 267 people are living. These people are paying an annual rent of £2,270. 18s. Some of these people have paid fifty times over for every inch of space they occupy. It is free houses they should have![10]

The Tory Council and the opposition Labour Party rejected Father O'Ryan's sound advice. Indeed, they pursued the opposite course. You were made to pay for your council house or flat ... through the nose!

The extent of the housing crisis in Liverpool was not new. Alderman Rutherford, the Tory chairperson of the Housing Committee, was inordinately fond of expounding on the 'cause' of the problem. It was the shape of the city, he argued, it crowded down to the rivers so that expansion could only take place in one direction – away from the river. But people wouldn't move from their work, whether dockers or rag-pickers, basket women or scalers. So for the Tories it was a problem without solution. Geography comes before people!

The city council was well aware of the seriousness of the problem. A report in the Architect's Journal in 1933 had argued that up to 50,000 new houses had to be built in Liverpool to overcome bad housing and overcrowding. 30,000 people were living in courts condemned as unfit eighty years previously. Another 6,000 insanitary dwellings were occupied and 700 cellars were illegally tenanted.[11] And in 1934 there were

Photo 8: Slum housing in Liverpool – a perennial problem for the poor.

24,000 people on the waiting list for council housing. The Medical Officer of Health for Liverpool, unlike his colleague from Bootle, recorded 13,069 houses as being 'ripe for demolition' in July 1933.[12] By September 1933, the Housing Committee accepted that they would have to build 15,000 houses to house slum clearance families alone.[13]

... And the Ugly

There was another attack on corporation housing which was to affect tenants as dramatically as higher rents. From 1925 onwards the Tory Government were continually eroding standards of house building. Houses with parlours and 950 square feet of space were common in the early nineteen-twenties. By the end of the twenties parlours were rare and space had been reduced. In the nineteen-thirties the average space of council houses was 620 square feet – a reduction of one third from ten years previously. Why had this happened?

First, it was yet another 'invisible' cut. Secondly, smaller houses were cheaper to build and demanded less subsidy from central Government. And thirdly, it was felt strongly that working class people should not be given the opportunity of good housing – it might give them ideas above their station. Or, as Lancelot Keay, Director of Liverpool Housing, put it,

> "I would prefer a well-planned estate with buildings of architectural merit, at a density of 16 to 20 an acre, than a development, such as may be seen in many towns, where every house enjoys its $1/_{12}$th of an acre and attempts to set an example of semi-detached respectability, but which is, in fact, a veritable blot on the landscape."[14]

And where did Keay (later to become Sir Lancelot Keay) live himself? In some grim little terrace or court off Scotland Road? No. He owned a 'veritable blot on the landscape' on Allerton Road!

In addition to Mr. Keay's aversion to building decent homes for working class people and the inability of people to pay the rents demanded, conditions were further eroded by the policies of the National Government elected in 1931. By the nineteen-thirties, the heroes of the 'homes fit for heroes' all had homes – or so the Government of the day would have them believe. After all, in Liverpool nearly 30,000 houses had been provided in the nineteen-twenties under the enabling legislation. The National Government, pursuing its attack on state spending and its ideological offensive on working class rights, decreed that it could no longer subsidise public housing. From 1933, all assistance from central Government to local councils to build houses for what were termed 'general needs' was terminated. Money was only to be available for two specific tasks, slum clearance and the eradication of overcrowding. State policy returned solely to curbing the 'sanitary problems' – back to 'Victorian values'.

In Liverpool the consequences of this policy were more dramatic than in many other areas. The council had recognised people's resistance to moving to the outskirts of town. People wanted to stay around the docks – not to live in slums, but to be near work or, more precisely, chances of work. Time after time reports, surveys and deputations reiterated this point. After 1933 the council had no chance of extending the outer estates, but attention had already shifted to the 'inner city'.

Slum Clearance

The Greenwood Act of 1930 introduced by the Labour Government strengthened the development of tenement building. It was based on a recognition that housing policy had to rectify specific problems of slum housing, particularly those facing the unemployed, the casually employed and single parent families. Take the example of a house in Rock Ferry in 1927 in which eight families of fifteen adults and fourteen children lived. A court hearing revealed that the landlord failed to keep the house 'in a good state of repair', despite receiving a weekly rent of £4 5s.[15] The Greenwood Act tried to tackle this kind of abuse, both by the introduction of subsidies to enable councils to build directly for tenants whose homes were to be demolished, and by reviewing the legal powers of landlords to facilitate slum clearance.

Ever since 1869, when the council had built St. Martin's Cottages, tenements had been put up in the dockside areas, paid for on the rates. It was always seen as a way of modifying the 'rowdyism' of the people – housing as a form of social control. But after the First World War advocates of flats in the dockside areas came from all political parties. The first big developments, like Melrose House, Dingle House and Gerard Gardens, came as a direct consequence of visits to Hamburg and Vienna by Tory and Labour representatives from the council. Or at least the designs were *based* upon European models. When the scheme to build

Photo 9: Gerard Gardens as it appeared in 1937, one of the tenement blocks built in the thirties – and recently demolished.

Photo 10: The Minister of Health (on swing, centre), at the opening of another tenement block, Myrtle Gardens – sold off in the eighties for private development.

Gerard Gardens was submitted in 1930 there were to be four wings in an 'X' shape, ten stories high, housing 400 families with a creche on the roof. Billy Robinson, speaking for the Labour Party, commented,

> "Having just returned from Hamburg, where they have five or six storey buildings, I am terrified to think what ten storey tenements would look like in Liverpool. And even with a lift it is doubtful whether some of the little children would ever go downstairs."[16]

As the plans moved from the drawing board to the building site, Gerard Gardens lost its radical pretensions. The first casualty was the creche. Then the central heating system was dispensed with, then the playground in the middle, then the lodging rooms for single people and finally, there was to be no communal restaurant as planned.

One month beforehand there had been a sharp exchange between Hugo Rutherford, the pontificating chairperson of the Housing Committee, and Hall Caine, the Labour M.P. for Everton. Rutherford argued that the new tenements were 'much better' than their Viennese cousins. Hall Caine reminded Rutherford that 'Red Vienna' provided, in their tenements, playgrounds, libraries, lecture halls, day nurseries, steam laundries, drying rooms, swimming pools, showers and a gym. Where were these facilities in Kirkdale, the Dingle and in Gerard Gardens? Caine criticised the housing policies of Tory Liverpool and added, prophetically,

> "... the type of unsightly tenements now being built will be the potential slums of the future."[17]

Two Classes of Tenants

How was it to be decided who lived where? The chairperson of Prescot Urban Council left little room for doubt. Twelve applicants had to be selected out of 230 for new council housing in Prescot. He argued,

> "... there are probably 60 names on the list which may reasonably be put before the meeting. But there are others whom I would not allow to go into pigsties. It is a very important matter as to the class of tenants we allow to go into our houses.[18]

You may be forgiven for thinking that this man had built the houses with his own hands and his own money. So much for people's housing.

In Liverpool other factors were to be taken into account. In 1930 the Housing Committee had laid down the basis for the selection of tenants:

"1. Tenements in cleared sites ... to be limited to the accommodation of that number of the displaced tenants who, having regard to their occupation, it is considered essential to be rehoused on or near the sites of their present accommodation.

11. Accommodation for all persons likely to remain unemployed pending the development of new industry and whose livelihood is not dependent on continued residence in their present neighbourhood, to be provided in cottages on specially selected sites on the outskirts."[19]

If you had a job you were re-housed in the same area. If you were unemployed you were to be moved – to await the arrival of 'fresh industry'. So the demands of the dock employers for a flexible and accessible labour force were granted. The surplus would be moved to Speke or Huyton to provide labour power for those industrialists who were to be bribed to locate new plants on the outskirts of the city. Thanks to the Liverpool Housing Department there would be a ready pool of labour awaiting.

Ability to Pay

Tight checks were kept over who would be allowed to occupy corporation housing. In February 1932 the Housing Department laid down the following guidelines. To even qualify for registration prospective tenants had to prove "an ability to pay rents for houses suitable for their requirements"; their income had to be less than £7 a week; and they had to have been resident in Liverpool for five years.[20] This latter guideline effectively enabled disqualification and discrimination to be practised against those 'suspected' of being a recent arrival. Irish, African and Chinese people were viewed with suspicion under the regulation.

Four years later additional regulations were passed by the council. The first clause illustrated the continuing problem of housing shortage. It read, "no more application forms for council housing are to be issued". Clause three read,

"Applicants in receipt of public assistance or unemployment benefit were not to be considered ineligible if their current rent books showed their ability regularly to pay rents of not less than half the amount proposed to be charged by the Corporation."[21]

When regulations are meant to be unclear the double negative is often used. In theory, unemployed people qualified for registration. However, the purpose of numerous provisions in regulations was to allow housing officers to practice maximum discretion. The unemployed consistently failed to secure council accommodation because of their supposed 'inability to pay'. How many tenants could produce rent books? Of those who could, how many could prove their ability to pay regularly? Pressures were put on women to go short so that the rent book might sustain the inquisition of the housing officer.

Whose Fault?

Lancelot Keay was the Director of Housing for Liverpool throughout the nineteen-thirties. He had the audacity to call his own home the 'Red House', not, we would add, because he was a friend of the working class. His vision of tenement housing and the creation of poverty-stricken outer estates illustrates that. But in a very real sense he was a prisoner of the system. Even before the arrival of the National Government housing was under attack. While public housing had grown in the nineteen-twenties in response to pressure from the working class, standards had been forced down. Council housing was not heavily subsidised so rents were high. And precisely who was eligible was also kept under close scrutiny.

The National Government added another ideological twist. Not only was central Government support cut but the housing crisis was claimed to have been solved. Any remnant of the problem could be safely channelled into the hands of the private builder. The thirties became the era of the owner-occupier. Massive, private semi-detached estates spread along the arterial roads, while for those left behind in the web of regulation and entitlement provision was at a minimum.

The Slums Remain

In the last few months of the second Labour Government the National Federation of Building Trade Operatives held a conference in the Picton Hall to herald the arrival of the Greenwood Act – the Slum Clearance Act. National Union Officials, church leaders and civic dignatories attended in droves. The banner behind the platform read, "No slums in fifteen years". It is not clear whether it was a pledge or a dream. The successes were charted – 19,000 council houses built in Liverpool since the war, with the opportunity to extend that record under the new act. Problems were alluded to. A plasterers' delegate criticised design and control on Norris Green – 1,748 ceilings had fallen in on the estate. Nevertheless, a general, optimistic motion was moved from the floor.[22]

There was one dissenting voice in all this self-congratulation, a certain Leo McGree, a well-known local Communist Party activist. He drew attention to the number of vacant houses in the Rodney Street district and moved an amendment urging the slum dwellers to take over and occupy vacant houses. The amendment, the *Daily Post* smugly reported, 'found no support'. Leo McGree was closer to the problem than the civic leaders. Tory Governments, then and now, had a vested interest in maintaining a housing shortage to boost their natural supporters in the private housing sector – slum landlords, money lenders and private builders – the people who make money out of atrocious housing conditions. Few could challenge that power, except those like Leo McGree and the National Unemployed Workers Movement who turned out to prevent the bailiffs from evicting tenants (see Chapter 12). This was one action that could materially benefit the housing situation of the unemployed when all around the doors seemed closed.

Notes
1. *Liverpool Echo*, 3.7.1935.
2. MSRG, interview with Jim Mottram.
3. *Liverpool Daily Post*, 2.1.1929.
4. *Daily Worker*, 19.9.1931.
5. *Liverpool Daily Post*, 28.2.1931, 24.7.1931.
6. *Liverpool Daily Post*, 23.2.1934.
7. *Liverpool Daily Post*, 11.8.1939.
8. *Liverpool Daily Post*, 4.10.1933.
9. Liverpool University Settlement, *Housing Problems in Liverpool* (1931), p.16.
10. *Liverpool Daily Post*, 2.10.29.
11. *Liverpool Daily Post*, 22.6.1933.
12. *Liverpool Daily Post*, 14.7.1933.
13. *Liverpool Daily Post*, 1.9.1933.
14. *Liverpool Daily Post*, 20.11.35.
15. *Liverpool Daily Post*, 23.7.1927.
16. *Evening Express*, 30.5.1930.
17. *Liverpool Daily Post*, 15.4.1930.
18. *Liverpool Daily Post*, 28.9.1927.
19. Liverpool Corporation, Housing Committee, *Minutes*, 27.11.1930.
20. Liverpool Corporation, Housing Committee, *Minutes*, 18.2.1932.
21. Liverpool Corporation, Housing Committee, *Minutes*, 16.1.1936.
22. *Liverpool Daily Post*, 2.2.1931.

PART TWO
CLASS RULE AND THE STATE

5

"GOD HELPS THOSE WHO HELP THEMSELVES": THE LAW, THE STATE, AND THE UNEMPLOYED

On 12th August 1927, twenty-five year old Alexander Phillips of Slater Street appeared in court charged with throwing a brick through the window of Woolworths in Church Street. He was married with a small child. He and his family lived on 22s a week, the relief payment from the Board of Guardians. The money, he claimed, "would only buy a cigar for Lord Birkenhead". The magistrate fined him £20, commenting, "God helps those who help themselves. Men who want to work and not to spout can often get work."[1]

A year later, twenty-seven year old Sarah Fleet was charged with abandoning her eleven month old twins in a busy park.

> "I did it in desperation because every door was closed against me and the guardians would not take the babies. All they could offer was the workhouse. I have had three opportunities of getting work but lost them all on account of the babies. I'm sorry I left them there."[2]

Such tragedies were commonplace in the nineteen-thirties. Dusty files remain the only testimony to the many victims of mass unemployment.

The sufferings of the unemployed were structured by the regulations of the numerous Unemployment Acts passed in the twenties and thirties. These laws, harsh enough in themselves, were made far worse by unsympathetic bureaucrats at local employment exchanges and Public Assistance Committees. Despite the apparently haphazard development of unemployment legislation a number of themes and ideas emerge. One question always asked, was "How much is it going to cost?", which fitted neatly into the financial orthodoxy of the period. Public expenditure should be as low as possible, particularly when it came to maintaining the unemployed.

In this respect, the new laws were direct descendants of the Poor Laws. The 'poor' fell into two categories, deserving and undeserving. As individuals, some people might be unemployed through no fault of their own, but for the majority unemployment was avoidable. These were the 'undeserving' poor, who must be taught the value of hard work and responsibility. Any money given by the State to maintain the unemployed was not a 'right', but a privilege, granted where there existed a 'genuine' desire to work. Workhouses were, of course, the ultimate test of the genuine worker. But as these were gradually phased out, so other tests were introduced to avoid unnecessary payments to the 'slackers' and 'scroungers'. As unemployment increased so support for such tests gathered momentum. More and more people found themselves in the 'undeserving' category. For them, benefit was only paid after the most rigorous and detailed investigation of their personal circumstances and intentions. The *means test* and other restrictive regulations attached to the payment of benefit were the workhouse by another name. The law was used not only to foster a particular ideology concerning the unemployed, but also to control, divide and weaken both the unemployed themselves and the working class as a whole.

"You Had to Fight to Get Anything"

Compulsory state unemployment insurance covered 12 million workers by 1920. Benefit was directly related to previous contributions in a ratio of one week's benefit to six week's contributions – the 'one in six' rule – and claimants could not draw benefit for more than twenty-six weeks in any one year. However, by 1921 the national unemployment rate had reached 15% and as the number of long-term unemployed rose, so more and more people were exhausting their right to benefit. Consequently, they became the responsibility of the local Board of Guardians. Since poor law relief was paid out of the rates, the aim of most Boards was to keep payments to an absolute minimum. The Guardian's means test was notoriously rigorous and degrading, as Ann Kelly remembers,

> "What I remember of the means test was the way you had to fight to get anything. And it was degrading to go and sit and wait for those people to decide whether you were entitled to 2 or 3 shillings. It humiliated people, it did. And all the questions they asked! If they came to your house, and you had any decent furniture, you were told to go and sell it, and to live on that money. You were pretty comfortable if you had anything like that. But half of them only had like an orange box or a log ... something like that."[3]

Even after such humiliation, the relief given to many families was not enough to prevent poverty, malnutrition and ill-health. In addition, those forced to 'go to the Parish' were subjected to intense social stigma.

The rapid increase in the number of long-term unemployed from 1920 onwards sent shock waves to Whitehall. The Government became increasingly alarmed by the rising number of demonstrations involving the unemployed. They were especially keen to contain the anger of ex-soldiers, many of whom had been unemployed since returning from the war. It was this set of circumstances that explains the introduction in 1921 of 'uncovenanted benefit', which was payable over and above a person's entitlement under the 'one in six' rule. Alongside this, a payment for dependents was introduced. These concessions raised the cost of maintaining the unemployed. Moreover, the Government feared that the changes might encourage 'malingering'. To avoid this, uncovenanted benefit was made discretionary, like parish relief. The long-term unemployed now had to appear before a Local Employment Committee. Thus the infamous 'means test' was introduced into the Insurance Scheme for the first time. Now every item of saleable personal property, as well as the income of relatives, would be taken into account in determining the level of benefit.

"Genuinely Seeking Work"

The means test, greatly resented in itself, was reinforced by another regulation which demanded that a claimant must be *'genuinely seeking work, but unable to obtain such employment'*. On the surface this regulation might have seemed innocuous, but it was implemented in such a way that its effect on the unemployed was devastating. It fitted neatly with the Government's view that certain sections of the unemployed were 'scrounging' off the state. Consequently, all claimants were rigorously questioned as to their efforts to find work. The unemployed were required to produce proof that they had visited factories and workshops, and were interrogated as to their location, means of transportation, and the results of their enquiries. Neighbours, friends and relatives were questioned about claimants' day-time activities, and the Investigating Officer of the Local Employment Committee frequently visited people's homes in the early hours of the morning. These were the first in a long line of professional snoopers. Their job was important because the Committee could recommend a refusal of benefit without having to prove that a claimant could have found a job. Those with bikes, as we know, were expected to go further afield in their search for work, but for most their experience was like Max Cohen's

"Day after day after day I walked the streets to the point of exhaustion, pursuing the baffling phantom of work."[4]

The short-lived 1924 Labour Government extended the test to apply to all applicants for the dole, as well as introducing another new rule which required claimants to prove that they had been in work for a 'reasonable' period in the previous two years to qualify. This was the first indication that the Tory Party was not alone in subscribing to the view that sections of the unemployed were not 'genuinely' out of work. The Baldwin Government of November 1924 consolidated this strategy, arguing that every effort should be made to ensure that only 'deserving' cases received money.

The application of these punitive regulations by unsympathetic bureaucrats sent more and more of the unemployed to the Guardians. In Liverpool, in the first two months of 1927 alone, nearly 6,000 people were disallowed benefit. Of these, two-thirds were struck off under the 'genuinely seeking work' clause, or because it was considered that they had not done enough work in the previous two years. Despite the fact that Employment Committees were local bodies, there was little opportunity for any leniency in the interpretation of the law. The Committees were carefully monitored by the Minister of Labour.

1927 – A Watershed?

The next major change in the Unemployment Insurance Scheme came with the introduction of the *1927 Unemployment Insurance Act*. The new Act followed closely the recommendations of a Royal Commission appointed in 1925 and chaired by Lord Blanesburgh. The Commission faced pressure from all sides. The Government wanted to see an end to the drain on the Exchequer which unemployment benefit had become. But this aim had to be balanced against the dissatisfaction of the unemployed with the conditions imposed upon claimants. Also they faced pressure from the locally run Boards of Guardians who were arguing for centralised responsibility for the long-term unemployed, in order to ease the burden on the local rates.

The Commission's proposal was to end the distinction between standard and extended benefit. They were to be merged into a single benefit of unlimited duration, payable only on condition that at least thirty contributions had been paid in the previous two years, or fifteen in one year.

The new Act, then, abolished the 'one in six' rule, but the thirty contributions rule meant that claimants would have to have had at least seven and a half months employment in the last two years to qualify for benefit – a condition which many of the unemployed could not satisfy. In recognition of this the Government were forced to introduce a new benefit called 'transitional benefit', payable to those who could show either that they had made eight contributions to the unemployment insurance scheme in the previous two years, or thirty contributions at any time. Although the introduction of transitional benefit did not square with the principle of balancing incomings and outgoings in the Insurance Fund, the Commission had, for some unspecified reason, calculated that the average unemployment rate would soon settle down to around 6% and therefore argued that the new benefit would only be a temporary measure. In fact, the Government were forced to extend transitional benefit every year, and by 1930 about 10% of the unemployed were receiving it.

Old Enough to Fight

Perhaps the most significant aspect of the 1927 Act was its penalisation of the young unemployed and women. Previously, everyone over eighteen was paid the adult rate of benefit. Under the new Act the rate of benefit for men over twenty-one was reduced from 18s to 17s, for women over twenty-one it remained at 15s, but in the eighteen to twenty-one age range men had their benefit cut to 10s and women to 8s. This was a sudden and drastic reduction in the income of the young unemployed. It marked the beginning of a strategy, to be followed by subsequent Governments, of attacking specific sections of the unemployed; a strategy which created divisions within the unemployed and prepared groups of workers to accept low paid jobs in the future. These policies were justified in a number of ways. The Tory view which underpinned the legislation was expressed unequivocally in parliament,

"I think it is now a matter of comment throughout the country that this juvenile unemployment pay is one of the most disgraceful things ... the less the younger element can be brought up to believe that they may be able to live either on unemployment pay or charity of some kind the better it will be for the moral feeling of this country. The first aim of the Minister by this Bill is to do away with the dole"[5]

In the debate, many Labour M.P.s argued that the cuts would have a particularly devastating effect on young single women, more and more of whom might be forced into prostitution. Whether or not this occurred is impossible to tell, but certainly the cuts in benefit pushed women to take work as low paid domestic servants. 8s a week could not even pay for a rented room. As Ellen Wilkinson argued,

> "I know there are many supporters of the right Honourable Gentleman who imagine the whole problem of the employment of women is solved by saying "let them go into domestic service" ... Say the girl is a milliner and is out of work for a couple of months ... With these girls it is not a question of taking up an entirely new career in domestic service ... They wish to remain in their trade and their trade needs them ... I say quite frankly that we have no right to tell girls in that position, any more than to tell men, that they must change their occupation ... Take the case of the girl living in lodgings ... Who is going to keep a young woman of 18 to 21 years of age for 8s a week ... I cannot too strongly stress the tragedy this is going to mean to girls in our great cities."[6]

What could not be ignored, however, was that three Labour M.P.s had signed the Report and conceded to its recommendations. Margaret Bondfield, later to become Minister of Labour, was one, for which she soon won the nickname 'Eight-bob-a-week-Maggie'. In attempting to justify her support for the cuts, she argued that they were appropriate when combined with facilities for training the young unemployed. It was a thin argument, particularly when her view of training became clear. Training for what? was the obvious question. This was her answer,

> "You cannot get these people into industry unless you set up a comprehensive nationwide system of training. You may call it what you like. I do not care for a moment what you teach inside the training centres. You can teach them algebra, geography, dancing or singing. What you have to do is to bring them into a position where they will have occupation for the mind and proper physical exercise and care for the body. I know of no training scheme that I have approved that does not make part of the scheme a properly cooked mid-day meal. In connection with the women, it is part of their training. When they cook a dinner they eat it."[7]

Training, then, was to be nothing more than a meal ticket and an opportunity to encourage the 'right' attitude amongst the young. Keep people dancing, singing and cooking, keep them off the streets, deny them a decent level of benefit and the problem of youth unemployment is solved. This despite the fact that, as George Buchanan, the Clydeside M.P. and one of the few consistent opponents of the administration of unemployment insurance throughout the twenties and thirties, commented, "They were old enough to fight for you". In the nineteen-thirties they were to be classed as children and denied their independence and hopes for the future. By 1940 many would be soldiers again.

"To Apply Equally to Both Sexes"

The new Act was also designed to encourage a more strident use of the *genuinely seeking work* clause. The Government felt that this clause was too vague. How could the genuine claimant be distinguished from the scrounger? According to the Blanesburgh Commission,

> "In considering whether a person is genuinely seeking work the most important fact to be ascertained is the state of the applicants mind."

Did this mean that the Employment Exchanges would have to employ residential psychiatrists? No, the matter was far simpler. The Commission used the ruling from a contemporary appeal case to clarify the situation and set down the statutory principles of the regulation. It stated,

> "An applicant who is genuinely seeking work should generally be able to show that besides registering for work at an exchange, she is making personal efforts on her own behalf to find work and is not content merely to wait until it is thrust on her. Moreover, she should be able to satisfy a Court of Referees that she is not merely looking for a particular kind of work which is congenial to her or to which she has been accustomed, but that she is also trying to get other kinds of suitable employment if there are any for which she is qualified."

The recommendation, to *apply equally to both sexes*, obscured the reality. Women, particularly those who were married, were prioritised for investigation.

As early as 1923 the Liverpool Trades Council and Labour Party had protested to the Labour Exchange about the practice of suspending from benefit women who had served an apprenticeship but who were refusing, when unemployed, to take work as domestic servants. Not only was domestic service outside the unemployment insurance scheme, thus eliminating the possibility of future claims, it was also a job despised by many women. By 1927, it had become clear that unemployed women, whatever their previous trade, were being systematically harassed into domestic service on the pretext that unless they accepted this work they were not genuinely seeking work.

Organised opposition to the 'genuinely seeking work' test had begun in 1925 among Clydeside workers. But on the whole, the Labour movement was extremely sluggish in taking up the issue. It was not until 1929 that the National Unemployed Workers Movement took it up and established its repeal as the main slogan of a national hunger march. This quiescence is partly explained by the fact that it primarily affected women. After all, many male trade unionists viewed women as unnecessary competitors in a diminishing labour market. Because there was no automatic recognition of women as genuine wage earners, state harassment of women into domestic service was often not seen as an infringement of rights.

A Deaf Ear to Suffering

The 1927 Act set the pattern for the treatment of the unemployed in the thirties. More and more of the unemployed were seen by the middle-class, and M.P.s in both parties, as undeserving scroungers. Particular groups, such as women and young people, were singled out as parasites, bringing the insurance scheme into disrepute. In fact the very groups of workers experiencing the greatest difficulty in finding new jobs became the scapegoats for the bankrupt insurance fund.

By 1927, another factor had clearly emerged in the determination of benefit levels. While Poor Law Relief remained below unemployment benefit levels, from the point of view of the state it was also important to further maintain a gap between these levels and the lowest wage rates. This was put quite clearly in the debates on unemployment insurance that took place in Parliament,

> "One of the governing factors of our present system of unemployment insurance is that we do not want to get as good benefits as we can; one of the governing conditions is that the benefits must not be more than the general labourer's rate of pay ... if you have a flat rate of benefit low enough not to tempt the unskilled type of workman into unemployment rather than into work."[8]

Since it was assumed that higher benefits would encourage the malingerer, people's real needs in terms of diet, housing and good health were of secondary importance to the overriding aim of pressurising the unemployed into acceptance of low-paid jobs. For this reason, the state turned a deaf ear to the barrage of evidence concerning the extent of poverty, ill-health and malnutrition amongst claimants. The unemployed were the foundation upon which the 'road to recovery' of British capital was to be built.

The Bureaucrats Step In

The formation of Public Assistance Committees to replace the old Poor Law in 1929 was one step in the Government's programme for reforming benefit administration. From the early twenties the stated aim was "improved efficiency". Local political control, which was undermining this strategy, was to be neutralised. The first attempt to achieve this had been the Board of Guardians [Default] Act of 1926. Particular Boards had been characterised as 'extravagant' in their relief payments. The Act allowed the Minister of Health to dissolve an existing Board and to replace it with state appointed bureaucrats. Further legislation pursued similar objectives. The Local Authorities Act of 1928 allowed for increased intervention by the central authorities. Up and down the country Ministry of Health Inspectors and Auditors were sent to examine the administration and books of the Poor Law Authorities. The message from Westminster was that cuts had to be made. Relief payments had to be reduced and standardised. The inspectors had all the enthusiasm of missionaries.

The relief payments of the Guardians, always a few shillings less than unemployment benefit, were rarely made in cash. Tokens were given to be exchanged for food in specified shops. Thus was created the stigma of being 'on the parish', a stigma which outlasted the thirties. But the Ministry wanted more.

In 1928, when an inspector visited Birkenhead he expressed "grave concern" at the administration of the poor law. Money was being handed out, he claimed, to people who were not destitute, and furthermore to people "who didn't want to work". He suggested a greater use of 'institutional relief', a euphemism for the workhouse, in order to weed out non-genuine claimants. But, as in many other areas, this proved impractical. Workhouses were decaying, ancient institutions, structurally unable to deal with a large influx of new 'inmates'. The inspector's other solution was 'test work' – cheap, compulsory labour on public work schemes. But jobs still had to be found. In Birkenhead, the council could only come up with work for a handful of labourers digging the garden at the Tranmere Institute. The Guardians agreed to look into it. They cut relief payments; a single person's weekly payment fell from 12s to 10s. But few received this maximum, since the Means Test disqualified most.

Birkenhead was, in some respects, one of the more enlightened Boards. Labour members had won a few reforms over the years. West Derby Union, the authority for Liverpool, was, by contrast, anything but benevolent. However, surprisingly, the Inspector who visited in 1929 accused it of 'extravagance'. The true-blue response of the Guardians was to increase their rigour. But they faced problems. The chairperson lamented,

"We have been making every effort to get the local authorities to provide useful work, but the response is disappointing. Three years ago the Liverpool Corporation did take on 400 men for a short time, but since then there has been nothing."[9]

There were, quite simply, no jobs. The Guardians were, in fact, overwhelmed by the number of unemployed dependent upon them. As their reply to the Inspector stated,

"In one street consisting of 80 houses there are 187 families in receipt of relief. 104 of these require assistance directly as a result of unemployment."[10]

The total number of people dependent on relief payments in March 1929 was 56,000 in the West Derby Union. In two districts of the city, one person in five was dependent on the Guardians and in another three districts the ratio was one in six. 11,000 of these claimants were receiving benefits solely on the grounds of destitution due to unemployment.

A spirit of stringency and cost-cutting, strongly directed by central Government, pervaded most P.A.C.s. They proved as rigorous as their predecessors, and applied the Means Test mercilessly. The district auditor became a regular visitor, and every item of expenditure was checked and re-checked with relentless efficiency.

The Thirties – Life on the Dole

By the nineteen-thirties, the unemployed were familiar with life on the dole. They were used to being blamed, harassed and penalised for being the victims of 'the market'. In May 1930, a Liverpool woman wrote about her experiences at the Labour Exchange,

"I can give you some idea of the treatment of unemployed women in Liverpool. At the Labour Exchange the women are not permitted to take their babies. Notices are posted on the walls to this effect: 'Babies are not permitted upstairs' 'Babies are not allowed in here' 'Silence!' and so on. Just lately a few chairs have been brought in to allow the women and girls to rest while they wait, but only about twenty, a mere fleabite for the thousands that sign on.

All girls must have uniforms if they wish to start at the seaside resorts, and many girls cannot take a season's work because, being factory girls, they had not been able to buy the uniform of slavery.

The treatment at the PAC is even worse. The women and girls are simply seething with anger over these conditions and some of them say if the authorities do not do something soon they will start looting the shops!"[11]

By this time the campaign led by the N.U.W.M., on the nature of un-employment legislation and the treatment of claimants at the exchanges was gathering momentum. Margaret Bondfield, as Minister of Labour for the Labour Government, had made no secret of her view that certain sections of the unemployed were not *genuinely seeking work*. But in the face of widespread opposition to the genuinely seeking work clause from a significant section of the labour movement, she was forced to set up another parliamentary committee to head off this discontent. Sir Harold Morris was the chairperson, and his views were incorporated into the 1930 Unemployment Insurance Act, even though the committee was not unanimous. The new Act repealed the '*genuinely seeking work*' clause by shifting the responsibility for proving availability for work from the claimant to the Labour Exchange. The latter was obliged to notify a claimant of any vacancy and, if refused 'without good cause', benefit was disallowed. This change in the law was coincidental with a sharp increase in the numbers successfully claiming transitional benefit, particularly married women. Margaret Bondfield viewed this with alarm,

"I have definitely come to the conclusion that there is a body of opinion which believes that there is an evil here that ought to be cured. I think it will have to be made clear that benefit is not a dowry on marriage on account of contributions paid; that it is not a source of income to enable a woman to be economically independent of her husband's earnings, or to supplement the poor earnings of her husband; that marriage does not create a special privilege to escape the normal obligations of a job; that benefit is only due to an unemployed married woman who is still in the insurance field and will remain so in the same sense in which a man or a single woman remains."[12]

Bondfield had no need to look further than across the floor of the House of Commons to find allies to condemn this 'evil'. Men were to be upheld as the only genuine breadwinners after marriage, and women were defined as the legal and financial dependants of men. Once again, arguments in favour of 'moral rectitude' were used to justify the pragmatism of economic cuts.

This was increasingly necessary since transitional benefits were a permanent drain on the Exchequer, and unemployment continued to rise. Yet another Royal Commission was set up to investigate so-called 'abuses' and 'abusers' of the Unemployment Insurance Fund. Giving evidence to this Commission, Marion Phillips, Secretary of the Joint Standing Committee of Industrial Women's Organisations, argued,

> "I do not see any grounds of justice at all for these proposals to cut a woman off from insurance when she marries, and I can only suppose that they come from a very general idea that when you are in any industrial difficulty, if you can throw the burden of it on women, do so, and especially the married woman. It does not seem to me to have any sort of basis of justice at all."[13]

This was an isolated view. However much the evidence contradicted the allegation that women were abusing the scheme, the majority of the Commission had decided from the outset that they were a 'special case' who would no longer be covered by the scheme.

The repeal of the *genuinely seeking work* clause had, to some extent, improved the situation for all those signing on. But it amounted to little more than a saving in shoe leather. Painstaking and stringent investigation of claims remained constant.

Women: The Scapegoats

Between September 1927 and September 1930, the official unemployment rate amongst men had risen from 10.9% to 18.9%. In the same period, women's unemployment had gone up from 6.3% to 18.1%. The reason was quite simple. The depression was by then severely affecting industries in which large numbers of women were employed. The cotton industry was particularly badly hit, creating long-term female unemployment. This led to a dramatic increase in the number of women claiming transitional benefit. The depression had also accentuated the practice of sacking women on marriage, and they were invariably at the head of the queue in any redundancy programme.

Using a logic unique to Whitehall, the Commission turned the evidence on its head. Their report argued, firstly, that, because there was a growing practice of dismissing women on marriage and a reluctance by employers to take on married women, it was therefore unlikely that they would be able to secure an insurable job in the future. Secondly, it suggested that even those women who might want to work and who lived in regions where there was a likelihood that they could get a job, would often be prevented from doing so because of their responsibility for child care. Thirdly, the majority of women had, in the past, chosen to leave work when they married. For these reasons, the report considered that,

"in the case of married women as a class, industrial employment cannot be regarded as the normal condition."[14]

As one of the conditions for receiving benefit was 'normally in insurable employment' the scheme should not be expected to provide cover for them.

On this basis, the Anomalies Act was passed in July 1931. Margaret Bondfield, setting aside her feminist past, gave it her full backing. Unemployed married women would no longer receive benefit on the same basis as other workers. Their previous contributions to the unemployment insurance fund were now irrelevant. Unemployed married women would have to get a job after marriage in order to re-qualify. On Merseyside, and in many other parts of the country, it was a formidable, near impossible task. Women, already marginalised in the labour market, were now penalised at the dole office. By mid-November 1931, 3,000 Liverpool women had been disallowed benefit. They and their families had lost an indispensable source of income.

The Anomalies Act similarly attacked seasonal workers and those who worked a few days a week. More often than not these were women, like those who worked the summer in hotels on the Lancashire and North Wales coast, or those in the jam factories, taken on for a few months and then laid off. These were women who, the Chairman of the 1931 Royal Commission argued, said to themselves

"'I am going to supplement the income of my husband by working three or four months during the summer season, and thereafter I am going to rest at home'...but they would be entitled to receive benefit for the whole of the rest of the year.'"[15]

Nationally, by April 1933, 299,903 claims had been refused under the terms of the Anomalies Act. 250,920 of these were married women. The Labour Government had initiated a major attack on women's rights, ex-

Photo 11: A seasonal worker harvesting on a Maghull farm in August 1932. It was this kind of worker that was hit by the Anomalies Act of 1931.

ploiting a weak link in the labour movement. It was a time-honoured tactic, and heightened divisions between working class men and women throughout the period of economic crisis.

Cuts Bleed!

In August 1931, yet another Government committee was set up. Its brief was to produce proposals for reducing Government expenditure. Presided over by Sir George May, it forecast a budget deficit of £120 million a year, and placed its main emphasis on the charge to the Exchequer of the £30 million transitional benefit and £40-50 million deficit on the Unemployment Insurance Fund. To meet the deficit, the May committee proposed to raise another £24 million in taxes and to cut public expenditure by £96 million. Two-thirds of this was to come by slashing unemployment pay. The proposals were ruthless. Benefits were already miserably low. Further cuts must have echoed like a death-knell in the ears of the unemployed.

These recommendations were followed by splits within the Labour Government, and the formation of the National Government, led by Ramsay MacDonald. The Government moved quickly, and by September the National Economy Act was law. Benefit was reduced from 17s to 15s 3d for a single man, and from 15s to 13s 6d for a single woman. Dependants' allowances were cut. The Anomalies regulations were tightened and applied more rigorously. Employers and workers were to pay higher contributions, and standard benefit was paid for only twenty-six weeks a year.

But perhaps the most crushing defeat for the unemployed was the reintroduction of the means test into *transitional benefit*. Retitled transitional payment, it was paid through the Employment Exchanges as before, but now it was administered by the local Public Assistance Committees. This was a political rather than an administrative decision. The P.A.C.s were budget balancers par excellence. The long term unemployed would be classified and treated as paupers.

The unemployed were forced to adopt a new urgency in their search for work. By January 1932 there were 2,855,000 registered unemployed in Britain. Almost a third of them were now registered for transitional payments. Nearly a million were under scrutiny, in order to ensure not the slightest overpayment. The means test operated on the basis of household, and sons and daughters were expected to keep their unemployed parents. Chairs, clocks and carpets suddenly became saleable luxuries rather than necessities. Between 12th November 1931 and 23rd January 1932, 193,542 men and 77,995 women were cut off by the means test.

The degree of ruthlessness with which the P.A.C.s applied the means test depended to some extent on their political complexion. In a few Labour controlled areas, there was a leniency which offered a glimmer of hope to the unemployed. In Liverpool this was not the case. In April 1930 the powers and duties of the old Boards of Guardians had been transferred to the county and county borough councils, each of which formed a P.A.C. In effect little had changed. The P.A.C. in Liverpool carried with it the personnel and principles of the infamous West Derby Union Board of Guardians. Relief was only given on proof of complete destitution.

Centralisation

In 1934 the Government achieved its goal of many years when it took over the payment of all unemployment benefit. The Unemployment Act of 1934 set up two new bodies, the Unemployment Insurance Statutory Committee, which was to oversee the solvency of the unemployment insurance fund and propose changes in the rate of benefit, and the Unemployment Assistance Board (UAB) a centralised poor law authority, which took over the payment of relief to all those previously dealt with by the P.A.C.s. It was a measure designed primarily to take the burden of maintaining the unemployed off the local authorities (and hence the local rates) but also to remove, once and for all, any possibility of local deviation in the level of benefits paid. The new law preserved the distinction between the short-term and long-term unemployed, and although the cuts of 1931 were restored, the hated means test remained.

Between January and March 1935, the P.A.C.s were gradually superceded by the new U.A.B.s. The significance of the legislation now became clear. Many found that the new scales were less than the old poor law relief. Mass demonstrations led by the NUWM took place throughout the country with such intensity that the Government were forced to pass a 'Standstill Act', which allowed for the payment of either the old rates or the new ones, whichever was the greater. But it was only a partial victory for the unemployed. Despite the spontaneous solidarity shown in opposing the new rates, the means test remained intact. For the unemployed the creation of the U.A.B. reduced the possibility of local action and pressure affecting the rate of benefit paid. When, in 1935, demonstrators marched to local P.A.C. officers they were too late. Control of the purse strings had already passed into the hands of a remote centralised bureaucracy hidden in the bowels of Whitehall.

Forced Labour

The new Act had also introduced a new method of penalising the long-term unemployed. Single men and women, and married men up to the age of 35 found that transitional payments were conditional upon compulsory attendance at residential or non-residential labour centres, dubbed 'slave camps' by their critics.

For some time prior to this, it had been suggested that the unemployed spent too much time malingering on street corners. Benefits conditional on 'useful work', could remedy this. Test work on corporation schemes had already been attached to poor law relief from the early twenties. But now new projects were established. Initially, these were aimed at the young unemployed, and all sixteen to eighteen year olds claiming Guardian relief were forced to attend unemployment classes. Youth unemployment was a massive problem on Merseyside. The practice of sacking boys and girls at the age of eighteen, when the full adult wage became payable, had created a generation of 'unemployables'. Unemployment classes, teaching basic woodwork and domestic science, were passed off as training centres. In practice they did little more than keep people off the streets, since any skills acquired had little value in a city without jobs. The experience of this Liverpudlian girl is instructive,

"For some time now, on and off, I have been on short time and in order to draw benefit for the days I am unemployed (I've been paying insurance for nearly two years) I must attend the training school at Walton Road. About 300 girls attend in the morning, and a fresh batch, about the same number, in the afternoon, The 'training' we receive is as follows: Sums, English, Singing, Cookery and Laundry. I think the laundry teacher goes around all her family for the washing.

Any late-comer is stopped a day's pay – 1/3d . One girl was pretty sure of a job but was afraid to go after it for fear she would be late and so have her day's dole stopped.

Girls have been told to wash the powder from their faces and have actually been sent home, with consequent stoppage of benefit, because the principal thought that all the powder had not been removed.

A notice is pinned up in every classroom drawing our attention to the fact that five girls have had their benefit stopped for six weeks as 'punishment' for a breach of the rules. The girls in question were smoking in the lavatory during the break. It is as good as a picnic in the laundry class, watching the girls ironing and folding the garments, every little crease is ironed out, they are folded oh so very correctly. Failing to do this could be a breach of the rules."[16]

The Salvation Army also stepped in to 'train' the young. Schools of domestic service were set up for girls, and boys learnt basic farm work. After short courses the children were shipped off to Canada and Australia on liners commissioned by the Salvation Army to pre-arranged jobs. Emigration became a very popular way of reducing the unemployment figures. In 1928 the Liverpool Education Authority set up its first farm training centre, to prepare boys for life on the prairie. In the same year the Industrial Transference Board, a Government body set up to encourage migration from the depressed areas, organised a scheme for single men to undertake harvesting work in Canada. On 10th August, 3.000 men set sail from Liverpool with the promise of high wages across the Atlantic.[17] By the end of September most had returned. One man said that he had received better treatment as a prisoner of war. They had found on arrival that there were no jobs, and that wages were abysmally low. They issued a protest pamphlet on the Liverpool docks, which began,

"We have been the victims of a huge conspiracy of international capitalism to get rid of us from Britain. A conspiracy that has been entered into by the Tory Government of Britain and the Liberal Government of Canada. We are only the first contingent of a great scheme to rid British capitalism of its contradictory evils."[18]

The Grim Reality

As the thirties progressed, thousands of men and women were to leave their families and friends in search of work on the other side of the world. This was in one sense the 'ultimate solution'. Other schemes, such as the building of the East Lancs Road, and Otterspool Promenade, had little effect on the unemployment figures, benefiting only a few. Consequently it was left to all manner of voluntary organisations to deal with the everyday tragedies of unemployment. Co-ordinated by the National Council of Social Services, and supported by the Government, unemployed centres began to spring up in church halls and local clubs. But the NCSS was not known for its imagination. Physical exercise was the staple diet in these centres. The unemployed were to be fit if nothing

Photo 12 & 13: (12) Liverpool boys receiving training at the Farm Training Centre at Lathom, September 1928, prior to emigration to Canada to seek work. (13) In the same month, workers returning from Canada, having failed to find work, disembarking at Liverpool.

else. Despite the enthusiasm of well-wishers, philanthropists, and social workers, there could be no local 'solutions'. It may well be true that, as the Liverpool City Council motto has it, "God helps those who help themselves". But in Liverpool in the thirties, it must have seemed to many of those unemployed that even the deity had abandoned them to their fate.

Notes

1. *Liverpool Daily Post*, 12.8.1927.
2. *Liverpool Daily Post*, 20.8.1928.
3. MSRG, Interview with Ann Kelly.
4. M. Cohen, *I Was One of the Unemployed* (London, Gollancz, 1945), p.85.
5. *Hansard*, 9.11.1927.
6. *Hansard*, 9.11.1927
7. *Hansard*, 9.11.1927.
8. *Hansard*, 9.11.1927.
9. *Liverpool Daily Post*, 25.4.1929.
10. *Liverpool Daily Post*, 25.4.1929.
11. *Daily Worker*, 21.5.1930.
12. *Hansard*, 8.7.1931.
13. *Royal Commission on Unemployed Insurance* (HMSO, 1931), Minutes of Evidence, p.935.
14. *Royal Commission* 1931, Final Report, p.242.
15. *Royal Commission* 1931, Minutes of Evidence, p.101.
16. *Daily Worker*, 7.3.1931.
17. *Liverpool Daily Post*, 10.8.1928.
18. *Liverpool Daily Post*, 15.9.1928.

Photos 14 and 15: Two contrasting images of the police in the thirties. (14) Two Wallasey police forwards foiled by the goalkeeper of the Wallasey Unemployed team, 1933. (15) Three Liverpool policemen arresting an anti-fascist demontrator, 1937.

Photo 15

6
POLICING THE SLUMP

In August 1932 the annual report of the Governor of Liverpool prison stated that, 'At present there appears to be an epidemic of gangs of idle unemployed youths who add to their dole by committing series of petty burglaries.'[1] In July 1933, when a Birkenhead man was sent to prison for four months for assault on the police, the magistrate commented that it had become the custom for the police to be set upon when arresting people 'in certain areas of the town.'[2] An article in the *Evening Express* in November 1935 written by a magistrate, John Loughlin (a one time Labour Councillor before joining the Tory party in 1933) complained of,

"The startling rise in the number of cases of hooliganism and assaults on the police in Liverpool ... Today the youth of the city is out of hand. Every night the police come into contact with lawless youth."[3]

Then as now, those who administered the legal system issued their dire warnings and labelled those most affected by the depression as criminals.

It needs to be said at the outset that criminal and lawless behaviour and actions are not objective concepts which are universally agreed. Crime is not a neutral word. What is considered criminal is essentially defined by the state and administered by police, magistrates and judges. The considerations of law define what is lawless. Sir John Ellerman, who died leaving £17 million, was not a 'criminal'; Jimmy O'Brien, who robbed his gas meter of 5/3d, was a 'criminal'. Policing is maintained in a framework which appears neutral, but is deeply partial.

When the resistance of the working class took a more organised and explicitly 'political' form then the partiality of the law and of policing was even more apparent. For example, in 1931 a series of marches held to present demands to the Liverpool Public Assistance Committee culminated in a march being violently dispersed by the police. Complaints of a police assault were made, but this was small beer compared to the four days of rioting in Birkenhead in 1932 following a police baton charge on an angry crowd outside the house of the PAC Chairman. The riots ended with a police attack on tenements in the town in which many people were injured. A few days later a mass demonstration in Liverpool condemned the actions of the Birkenhead police and rioting broke out as the march returned from the city centre.

Though the clashes in Liverpool and Birkenhead were the biggest until the large NUWM hunger march and demonstration in London in October 1932, there was fighting between unemployed demonstrators and the police also in Castleford, Bristol, West Ham and North Shields. Indeed, there were some months of that year when reports to the NUWM headquarters showed not a day passing without baton charges and arrests somewhere in the country. For the rest of the nineteen-thirties hunger marches and clashes with the British Union of Fascists provided regular reminders that the working class, whether in or out of work, was capable of more than purely individualistic responses to its predicament – and the police response was not usually perceived as impartial by the de-monstrators!

A Force of Scabs

When the new police force of the eighteen-thirties and eighteen-forties was founded its task was clear: the containment of the working class as a whole. At this time the growing agitation and political organisation among the working class posed a clear threat to the middle class. The Chartist Movement represented, from the late eighteen-thirties, the culmination and clearest expression of this challenge to the bourgeoisie. However, the threat was not seen in purely political terms. The very nature of working class life and culture was seen as something which needed to be brought under the control of the state. The police were to go into working class communities as 'domestic missionaries', not only to counter the political threat but also to monitor, control and reform people's daily lives.[4] From the point of view of the middle class, working class communities were islands of moral degeneration which provided a breeding ground for unrest, discontent and ultimately political agitation. The anti-police riots which occurred between 1839 and 1844 were the expression by the working class of their resistance to this interference in all aspects of their lives.[5] In fact, the resistance to the 'moral entrepreneurship' of the police continued after the riots ended in the constant skirmishes between police and people in working class communities.

Photos 16 & 17: Price Street, the morning after the Birkenhead Riots, 1932. Looted shops (above), and iron railings torn up in the battle (below).

This set the pattern of policing in the nineteenth century. In Liverpool, responsibility for policing initially lay with the Watch Committee, a body which represented, personally and politically, the interests of the merchant class. Over the following decades the Chief Constable gradually secured an increasing autonomy from the day to day control of the Watch Committee; but clearly his policies were established in the context of a city dominated by mercantile capital.[6]

By the inter-war period internal problems were developing within the police force which threatened the ability of the force to fulfil its established role. In August 1919 over one half of the Liverpool and Birkenhead police and three-quarters of those in Bootle went on strike over the decline, since 1900, in their real earnings, the unfairness of the promotions system and, the final catalyst of the strike, the Government's quashing of any hopes that the National Union of Police Officers would be officially recognised. The Union, which was affiliated to the TUC, Labour Party and Liverpool Trades Council, had grown rapidly on Merseyside since the successful strike of the police in London in 1918. However, lack of police support elsewhere and from rank and file trade unionists in Liverpool (who understandably felt very ambivalent towards the police union) led to the collapse of the strike after three weeks. The strikers, having all been sacked at the outset, 'respectfully begged' the Watch Committee to reinstate them. Having had no difficulty in recruiting scabs at higher rates of pay or in recruiting 2,000 temporary specials from among bank and other business employees, the Watch Committee refused to reinstate any striker.

Instead, the opportunity was taken to reconstruct the local police force with 'more suitable' recruits – for the most part ex-servicemen who had been demobbed in 1918, many of whom had had commissions during the war. Others were recruited from outside the locality. For example, in Bootle nine experienced constables were imported from Manchester and promoted to the rank of sergeant, and two-thirds of the new constables came from the Aberdeen, Dundee and Grampian regions of Scotland. The smashing of the growing police union movement was made possible (as was to recur with the implementation by the Tories of the Edmund Davies Report on police pay in 1979) by the passage of a Bill which increased pay and improved working conditions. As a result constables on maximum pay received over half as much again as the average male industrial worker throughout the inter-war period.[7] Clearly

average male industrial worker throughout the inter-war period.[7] Clearly the establishment of a well-paid scab police force could only reinforce the antagonisms which still lingered on as a consequence of police violence during the Transport Strike of 1911, as well as the police attack on unemployed demonstrators in and around the Walker Art Gallery in 1921.

These events took place against a backcloth of great militancy among the British working class and widespread fears among the ruling class that the Russian experience of 1917 was about to be emulated. One result of this and of the continuing unrest of the twenties and thirties, was a strenuous effort by the Home Office to further centralise policing policies and thereby to distance even further the possibility of local (socialist and communist) politicians influencing police behaviour.[8] Increasing financial dependence upon central government also reduced the power of the local Watch Committee. The result, however, was not just centralisation but yet greater autonomy for Chief Constables.

During the inter-war years Liverpool Watch Committee was controlled by the Tories, and efforts made by Labour politicians to question police policies and practices were not very successful. Any doubts held by the Tories as to the Chief Constable's policies tended to be negotiated informally. For the most part they could rest secure in the knowledge the Chief Constable knew his job – a professional. Certainly, he retained wide discretion to determine the priorities of policing. The police officer on the street, too, had wide discretion as to how he carried out his job. These factors, coupled with the inevitable, and frequently intentional, ambiguity of the law, meant that the police had great opportunities to use their powers selectively in the maintenance of 'order'.

Containing the Working Class

The working class of the twenties and thirties was by no means an homogeneous group. As we have seen, there were significant national, racial, sexual and religious divisions. In Liverpool, the Irish, black people, women and Catholics all suffered discrimination. But with respect to policing there was another important line of division – whether, how and where you worked was crucial in conditioning your experience of, and relations with, the police. A large proportion of the workforce (40-50%) were in port-based casual occupations where unemployment

quired by the ruling merchant class of Liverpool since the eighteenth century and which was now bearing the brunt of the trade depression. Casualism, aggravated by chronic unemployment, cemented the large 'informal' economy in which the struggle for survival led to frequent clashes with bourgeois notions of propriety. And it was these casual workers, and the dockside areas they lived in, which were a particular target for the Liverpool police. This is well-illustrated by the memories of one South End Docker:

"If you were standing on the corner when we came out of the pub ... they used to come along and say 'come on, move'. So we used to stand on the side because we weren't caus- ing an obstruction. The idea was if you were standing on the foot-path you were causing an obstruction, so we stood in the gutter and the sergeant would look and say, 'That's where you belong anyway. I'll still run you in, you're obstructing the traffic'. So you couldn't win there.

If you were walking three abreast or four abreast along the street, you know the way people do, especially in the summer, the policeman would just stop you and split you up. He'd say, 'Eh ...' and he'd come out with a mouthful. Doesn't matter who it was and he'd make you walk behind each other. They said you were obstructing the pavements. Prob- ably they were right at the end of the day, some bye-law or what have you, but they weren't people you could go to. People said that we treated them with respect but we didn't. We were afraid of them, we didn't respect them. Nine out of ten people were afraid, it was as simple as that."[9]

Policing Crime: Imposing Middle Class Morality

For 'street crime' the police had a whole battery of powers in the laws relating to obstruction, frequenting, betting and gaming, prostitution, va- grancy, breach of the peace, insulting behaviour and more. However, to use these relentlessly would have required excessive amounts of money and personnel and, because of community resistance, would have guar- anteed massive disorder. The slogan of 'law and order' which has al- ways been used by the Right in fact conceals a fundamental contradic- tion in the role of the police – enforcing 'law' and maintaining 'order' are often wholly incompatible. Efforts to enforce the law strictly fre- quently cause breakdowns in public order, while to maintain order the police must often ignore what is technically illegal.

Thus, different working class areas experienced differing levels of po- licing: in some the police adopted a lower profile, in others they main- tained a dominating presence. Outside working class areas, in commer- cial or suburban districts, police powers could be used freely against those who obviously did not belong there, to impose a kind of unofficial curfew on the working class.

The attempts by the police to impose bourgeois 'morality' upon the working class have historically been particularly focused on women. Giving evidence to a Government committee in 1927, the Chief Constable of Liverpool in effect defined all women alone on the streets as potential 'street offenders' as the following quotes indicate:

"The habits of the professional women have changed materially within the last decade. She is, from outward appearances, indistinquishable from others. Her manners are usually quiet and sober, her solicitation almost unobtrusive, and her room or flat occupied alone. She frequents licensed houses and places of amusement more often than the streets."

To the Chief Constable such women were 'depraved' but by contrast,

"The other class of similar street offenders who cannot be styled as depraved women, is mainly composed of irresponsible careless, ill-mannered young women and girls whose self-respect is lacking and who preen themselves for the purposes of attracting their contemporaries of the opposite sex, more for the sake of being treated to drink, refreshment or entertainment than for actual immorality. But such conduct is so risky that moral disaster often follows."[10]

Then, as now, the tone of police descriptions of the lives of prostitutes, and women in general, is a mix of moral condemnation and blatant sexism. The ideology of Victorian patriarchy and sexual hypocrisy was still intact in the depiction of 'fallen' women. Although writing about the second half of the nineteenth century, Judith Walkowitz's description is appropriate for the real situation in the nineteen-thirties.

"They were not rootless social outcasts but poor working women trying to survive in towns that offered them few employment opportunities and that were hostile to young women living alone. Their move into prostitution was not pathological, it was in many ways a rational choice given the limited alternatives open to them."[11]

Provisions of the 1921 Liverpool Corporation Act, police reports and occasional press 'campaigns' during the inter-war years attempted to impose an effective curfew on women unaccompanied by men since they were assumed to be prostitutes. Following press reports of an increase in convictions of women for drunkenness and of the 'custom in Liverpool public houses to request women to leave when they congregated at the bar in too great numbers',[12] the Liverpool Licensing Committee, in March 1927, objected to the renewal of five licenses in the North End on various grounds including an argument that 'the premises were frequented unduly by women'. Women were in effect being criminalised for either simply enjoying themselves or attempting to earn a living. This is clearly illustrated by a case which came up in the Liverpool courts in May 1930. Two women were claiming damages against four police officers for 'wrongful arrest and false imprisonment'. The women had been walking home from a dance and had stopped to talk to some men on the street at which point they were arrested and charged at the police station which the curious charge of 'annoying men'.[13] Unfortunately the outcome of their case is not reported but the fact is that women on the streets unaccompanied by men were a focus of police harassment.

A common manifestation of this was the police focus on the activities of street sellers in town. Occasionally, in response either to the promptings of local shopkeepers or their own superiors, the police would crack down and drive the sellers from the best pitches. It was women who had a particularly difficult time since flower sellers were at times prosecuted for prostitution rather than obstruction. Sometimes such police action brought forth protest from other quarters. In December 1931 the Liverpool Public Assistance Committee sent the following resolution to the Watch Committee:

"That the Public Assistance Committee regrets that the removal of the pavement pedlars from Church Street, London Road and other districts causes an increase in its expenditure and strongly recommends that the embargo that has been placed upon their activities should be removed so as to enable them to become self-supporting, and that the Watch Committee be informed accordingly."[14]

True to form, the Public Assistance Committee's real concern was to keep their expenditure as low as possible.

Throughout the thirties other aspects of working class life were subject to the moralistic attention of the police force; gambling was another 'crime' which they attempted to prevent. The difficulty of doing this was acknowledged at a meeting of the Royal Commission on Lotteries and Gambling in 1932. The police referred to the impossibility of stamping out street betting because most of the people had more sympathy with the gamblers than they did with the police. But, if as a consequence, gambling was often ignored by the police, occasional crackdowns were made both on the streets and in clubs. In August 1928, 129 men, mainly dock labourers, were convicted for betting after a raid on a club in Blundell Street. In 1930 the Chief Constable reported that a 'great many proceedings' had been taken against betting houses. 1935 brought another clamp down with forty-one Chinese appearing in court after a raid in Pitt Street in September and ninety arrested and charged after a raid on the Regent Members Club, Eberle Street in October. Such raids, however, frequently met with resistance: the one on the Mersey Members Social Club in Matthew Street, Bootle in September was greeted with an attack by 200 people armed with stones and bottles.[15]

Policing the Night

The self-appointed moral guardians in the Liverpool police also took it upon themselves to harass and raid gay meeting places. In 1935, for example, the owner and manager of a gay club – the "45" in Hanover Street – had been summonsed for permitting drunkeness, disorderly conduct and 'women of a certain class to meet together and remain on the premises'. The Stipendiary magistrate hearing the case was rather shocked. He said,

> "This is all news to me. Do you say there is a definite class of these young men in Liverpool? I have read something of the kind in London."[16]

Despite the defence claim that nobody complained about the club except the police when they appeared dressed as women with lipstick and powder, the defendants were found guilty of permitting disorderly conduct, while the other charges were dismissed. The 'pretty police' of the nineties have their own historical ancestors.

The other clubs which exercised the Chief Constable and his force in the thirties were ones owned or frequented by black people. In 1935, for instance, he wrote in his annual report:

> "One other club which was dealt with during the past year and which disclosed a particularly revolting state of affairs should be mentioned. The club was frequented by white, coloured and half-caste men and women. Nightly this place was the scene of excessive drinking, foul language, filthy conduct and dancing during which the grossest indecencies took place. Between and during the dancing indecent conduct between men and women was openly indulged in. The sanitary arrangements in this club were of the most primitive character."[17]

It is not wholly clear which aspect of the club most concerned the police – perhaps it was the racial mix, for it was during the inter-war period that paternalist white organisations became concerned at the problems of so-called 'half-castes' and perpetuated a number of racialist myths concerning interracial sex.[18]

In the same year the owner of the Hanover Social Club in Paradise Street, described in the *Liverpool Daily Post* as 'a meeting place of coloured men and white women' was fined £20 for keeping disorderly conduct and having no license. The stipendiary magistrate was alarmed by the 'large body of police' who had raided the club. A summons would have been sufficient he argued. However, black people successfully defended their right to meet and socialise in the teeth of such police opposition.[19]

City of Lawless Youth

Nevertheless, there was a clear attempt to persuade the public that there was a growing lawlessness. Much of the campaign focused on the young in a similar way to some of the 'moral panics' of later decades. The regularity of comments in thirties police reports regarding juvenile crime should do something to lay the myth that it is a phenomenon peculiar to the recent past. For example, in his 1932 report, the Liverpool Chief Constable recorded:

"Four children, aged 12, 10, 9 and 7 were kept under observation by the police for one evening and were seen to enter no less than 38 shops. Their method was to take parcels from the shopping bags or pockets of customers and then carry the stolen goods to their homes. It is alleged that this had been going on every night for about three months."[20]

And in 1936 he reported, "Since the year 1930 there has been a continuous increase in juvenile crime in the city".[21] He went on to criticise those who contested this point and claimed that since there had been continuity of police practice during this time his figures and conclusions must be correct. Since the 1933 Children and Young Persons Act had laid down new procedures it must be presumed that either the Liverpool police ignored it or that they had not been told about it!

The remarkable similarities in the tone and content of thirties police and press reports with those we are familiar with today suggests that little has changed. As was seen in Chapter 2, young people were particularly disadvantaged in the Merseyside labour market because of the problems of getting casual work on the docks or one of the few apprenticeships available elsewhere. This meant very high numbers of young people on the streets where they were particularly vulnerable to discriminatory policing.

Policing Politics
The state's last line of defence is the police, and whilst the policy of containment and regulation of the working class is a permanent feature, when confronted with collective action a more positive approach of surveillance and disruption is necessary. And when organised marches and demonstrations of workers and the unemployed took place outside working class areas they were even more threatening to the authorities. Such events were not always susceptible to control through the police's battery of street powers.

In strict 'legal' terms the Government was not in a strong position to prevent marches taking place. It needed to maintain the facade of liberal freedom. Nevertheless, any actions in the surveillance and dispersal of them could usually be dealt with by the use of some sufficiently all embracing charge such as 'breach of the peace' or obstruction. In practice, police behaviour was not subject to legal restraint, as with a march to hear Bessie Braddock address the National Unemployed Workers' Movement (NUWM) at Edge Hill.

"All I remember is getting hit in the back of the neck with a pair of those woollen gloves, police gloves, you know – nearly broke my neck. Specially when it'd been raining, they used to wear very, very heavy gloves and they didn't care for life or limb them police. The horses just run at you and that was it, they weren't bothered what you were or who you were."[22]

When it came to the large national hunger marches the state had more subtle, yet effective, administrative means to disrupt them. During the build up to the 1932 march the Ministry of Health sought to enforce the regulations against the marchers who used workhouses for overnight accommodation and food reserved for vagrants. The Ministry of Labour told local officials they should refuse the payment of unemployment benefit to marchers since they were not available to sign on for work. In an order from the Home Secretary to Chief Constables the police were told to assist officials in enforcing these regulations as well as sending back information to London regarding the numbers, movements, moods and intentions of the marchers.

The NUWM were able to combat the enforcement of some of these regulations much to the annoyance of the Government. A Cabinet Committee was set up to make recommendations to deal with this 'problem' and a bill to give the Home Secretary the power to prohibit marches was the result. This nearly became law until lawyers within the government argued that it gave the Home Secretary too much power.[23] In 1936 the passage of the Public Order Act did give the police greater power over the holding and route of marches.

The NUWM were not able to prevent considerable disruption of their campaign once the march arrived in London in 1932. Metropolitan Police files which became available temporarily in the early nineteen-seventies (they were hastily removed from public access) indicate that the police information came first from informers within the NUWM and second from plain clothes police attending meetings. There was at least one informer at a high level of the NUWM and others were in contingents of marchers. The information upon which Wal Hannington was convicted for incitement to disaffection after his Trafalgar Square speech in October 1932 came from police notes. Frequently police notes of meetings painted a vivid picture of the violent intentions of the marchers which were not borne out by subsequent events. Even when police action was successfully challenged in the courts – as with their raid and seizure of documents from the NUWM offices in 1932 – their prime objective, the disruption of the campaign, had been attained long before the case came to court.[24]

In the thirties, political disorder on Merseyside occurred both in the context of anti-fascist activity (See Chapter 11) and also in response to the extent of unemployment and the workings of the relief system (see Chapter 12). Faced with such organised opposition the police response often showed its most brutal and bloody side. A couple of examples demonstrate this.

In September 1931, 10,000 people marched to the Municipal Annexe in Dale Street to hear the result of a demand made the week before to the Public Assistance Committee for increased relief. By the time the march arrived the Finance Sub-Committee had left the building having rejected the demand. When a deputation emerged from the building to rejoin the march, mounted police and 100 foot police approached the procession and attempted to redirect it. There were scuffles before the

Photo 18

Photos 18 & 19: Scenes in Hyde Park of the 1932 hunger march. The marchers arriving to a tumultuous reception (left), and police on a control tower keeping a close eye on the crowd (above).

police broke the crowd into two sections – one being forced down Manchester Street where the crush was such that people were thrown through the plate glass windows of a shop. Eventually the march returned to Islington Square where it was violently dispersed by mounted police who then continued to break up any small gatherings on the pavements. Jack Hayes, the Labour M.P. for Edge Hill, raised the question of police behaviour in the Commons but without any great effect. A week later another large demonstration assembled with one demand – an immediate public inquiry into the actions of the police.

In this period the police also evolved new tactics in dealing with such demonstrations. In the 1932 riots in Liverpool a mechanised means of riot control was introduced. As armoured transit vans were driven into crowds in the riots of 1981, killing David Moore, so in 1932 combination bikes carrying five or six officers with batons were driven into the crowds. When close enough the police jumped off and charged while the remaining constable in the side-car laid into people as the driver pursued other demonstrators. This new procedure was apparently 'irresistible', but at least nobody was killed.[25]

Photo 20: Police on motorcycles about to go into battle against the unemployed in the Liverpool riots of September 1932.

But the force was not just restricted to Liverpool, as shown by this resolution which was presented to the Watch Committee.

"This mass meeting of Liverpool workers condemns the action of the Liverpool Chief Constable and Watch Committee for their connivance in sending Liverpool police over to Birkenhead to help baton down workers who were demonstrating against the starvation means test.

We recognise these methods of uniting the forces of capitalism as seen in the dispatch of police to Burnley district, as the attempt to break the fighting spirit of the workers by physical violence.

We demand the immediate withdrawal of Liverpool police from the Birkenhead and Burnley areas.

We call upon every worker, every Trade Union Branch and every worker's organisation to join with us in the demand."[26]

Strong criticisms of the police use of motor cycles, ostensibly purchased for the pursuit of car thieves (as was today's helicopter), were made in the Watch Committee. Five months later Jack Braddock spent three hours querying the budget estimates of the police as a result of events in September. After speaking of "the perfectly vicious police administration in this city" he questioned the use of fire tenders to carry police to demonstrations. Additionally, he called for a public enquiry into police behaviour and expenditure. When all this was defeated he called for a reduction in the police force and a 5% reduction in police expenditure.[27] On the same day Birkenhead Council received a petition from local residents complaining of recent police actions during the riots in which 417 windows had been broken – the police being solely responsible.[28] By means of surveillance and infiltration of working class organisations the state hoped to pre-empt any effective political action. But when this failed the police, locally and nationally, were quite prepared to break heads. In response to the organised campaigning of 1932 especially there was an increase in what would now be called 'positive policing'. On Merseyside, and elsewhere, baton charges were made as soon as it could be argued there was an 'obstruction', whether or not the crowd was disorderly. And in the major battles of 1932 across the country casualties among civilians outweighed those among the police by about 5:1. The policing of political opposition disclosed not only the coercive role of the police but also the beginning of a strategy of resistance to police powers.

In the Dock

The state in Britain has traditionally relied on the Justices of the Peace (magistrates) to deal with outbreaks of disorder. Their courts – then known as 'police courts' – were distinct from the Assizes and Quarter Sessions, now Crown Courts. They had the advantage of 'local knowledge' and could sit and mete out punishments quickly in the hope of deterring further disorder. They had the further 'advantage', and still do, of not involving juries which can be embarrassingly sympathetic with defendants in such cases. A typical sentence imposed by magistrates in Liverpool on people convicted of disorderly behaviour in the sectarian riots in July 1932 and in Birkenhead and Liverpool after the September rioting was a fine of £2 with the alternative of twenty-one days imprisonment. Since a fine of this amount was the equivalent of about three weeks benefit it was far from insignificant.

When more serious charges, such as unlawful assembly, incitement to riot, conspiracy to riot, or riotous behaviour were laid the case would have to be tried by a jury. If this was held locally then the chances of acquittal were higher – four out of twelve charged after the 1932 riots were acquitted at the Liverpool Assizes, and four out of six at the Birkenhead Quarter Sessions – than if the state shifted the trial to 'more reliable' areas. This was done with the 'ringleaders' of the Birkenhead riots, ten out of twelve of whom were found guilty at Chester Assizes and one, Leo McGree found guilty at Manchester Assizes. Even those found guilty by local juries were quite likely to be bound over, whereas all those convicted elsewhere were sentenced to terms of borstal or imprisonment, some with hard labour. The severest sentences were on Joe Rawlings, who got two years, and Leo McGree who got twenty months, both with hard labour. In Liverpool Jack Braddock was convicted of incitement and sentenced to six months but the conviction was quashed on appeal.

By the end of 1932, however, events on Merseyside and in London involving police surveillance and harassment, remands in custody, protracted trials in some cases and many terms of imprisonment had achieved the immediate objective of removing the most experienced leaders of the NUWM from the political scene.

Conclusion

In 1928 the Watch Committee of Liverpool authorised the purchase of bullet-proof body shields and portable arm shields "for use at close quarters on stairways or in passages".[29] Portable arm shields were clearly not intended to safeguard the contents of gas meters: these acquisitions signified a recognition by the Watch Committee that policing in Liverpool had an overtly political function in combatting "public disorder", and particularly that "disorder" associated with the organisation of the unemployed. In 1928, as well, the police deprived over 3500 people of their liberty, albeit temporarily, for drunkeness; over 600 for 'street obstructions and nuisance'; almost 600 for offences concerned with prostitution and further criminalised over 700 people for gaming and betting and 400 for begging, both being crimes without victims. Police regulated working class communities and working class lives to their standards of 'morality and order'. The unemployed once again bore a disproportionate weight of this burden.

Notes

1. *Liverpool Daily Post*, 31.8.32
2. *Liverpool Daily Post*, 25.7.33
3. *Evening Express*, 20.11.35
4. R.D. Storch, 'The Policeman as Domestic Missionary' *Journal of Social History*, IX:4, Summer 1976.
5. R.D. Storch, 'The plague of Blue Locusts: police reform and popular resistance in Northern England 1840-57,' *International Review of Social History*, 20, 1975, pp.61-92.
6. M. Brogden, *The Police: Autonomy and Consent* (London, Academic Press, 1982).
7. R. Bean, 'Police Unrest, Unionisation and the 1919 Strike in Liverpool', *Journal of Contemporary History*, 15, pp. 633-53.
8. I. Taylor, *Law and Order: Arguments for Socialism* (London, Macmillan, 1981).
9. Interview recorded with George Hughes.
10. Liverpool Chief Constable, *Annual Report*, 1927.
11. J.R. Walkowitz, *Prostitution and Victorian Society: Women, Class and the State* (Cambridge, Cambridge University Press, 1980).
12. *Liverpool Daily Post*, 10.2.27.
13. *Daily Worker*, 5.5.30.
14. Liverpool Watch Committee, *Minutes*, 29.3.32.
15. *Liverpool Daily Post*, 2.9.1935.
16. *Liverpool Daily Post*, 26.1.35.
17. Liverpool Chief Constable, *Annual Report*, 1935
18. I. Law, *History of Race and Racism in Liverpool* (Liverpool, Merseyside Community Relations Council, 1981), p.31.
19. *Liverpool Daily Post*, 6.3.35.
20. Liverpool Chief Constable, *Annual Report*, 1932.
21. Liverpool Chief Constable, *Annual Report*, 1936.
22. Interview recorded with George Hughes.
23. J. Stevenson & C. Cook, *The Slump* (London, Jonathan Cape, 1977), pp.218-20.
24. Ibid, pp.225-27.

25. Liverpool Watch Committee, *Minutes*, 27.9.32.
26. *Liverpool Daily Post*, 23.9.32.
27. *Liverpool Daily Post*, 2.2.33.
28. *Liverpool Daily Post*, 2.2.33.
29. Liverpool Watch Committee, *Minutes*, 26.6.28.

7
THE RICH AND THE POWERFUL: LIVERPOOL'S RULING CLASS

It seems to be a characteristic of the wealthy that they enjoy the embodiment of their wealth in physical form. It is not sufficient to *be* rich – one has to be *seen* to be rich. What more efficient way than bricks, mortar and open spaces. So, in Liverpool, public buildings, parks, monuments and street names have all been bequeathed by the wealthy, bearing testimony to their power: Holt House, Rankin Hall, Cunard Buildings, Holt Road, Stanley Road, Sefton Park, Bowring Park, Rathbone Buildings – the list is endless. Splendid testaments to the enormous wealth of Liverpool's 'worthies'. However, not all the wealth of the ruling class was of such respectable origins. Indeed, in the thirties, there were more than a few 'bad apples' in its ranks. Take the case of Lord Kylsant.

Lord Kylsant and the Slump
Lord Kylsant did not, in fact, hail from Liverpool, but his ambition and power was to be the source of much suffering in the city. An old Birkenhead seafarer recalls,

> When one of the White Star liners docked in Liverpool, coming back from the States, it was the custom that the stewards and stewardesses would take any left-over cakes, pastries and the like for their children. This one stewardess took a cake and wrapped it in a White star napkin.. It was a bit fancy...and cost 6d. She gets home – down off Scottie Road – and there's a knock at the door. Two bobbies. 'Can you accompany us to the Bridewell?'
> Down at Cheapside, she's charged with stealing....the napkin! In the court she's bailed out till the following Saturday. But ... come Saturday there's no sign of her. So they sent out a warrant for her arrest, went up to her house and break the door down. She's hanging there ... dead. Yes, I remember Lord Kylsant ... the most hated man in Liverpool[1]

Lord Kylsant owned, among other things, the White Star Line. He was born in 1863, into an aristocratic family in Pembrokeshire. Not that he was Welsh. He claimed to be able to trace his family back to Maximus, the Roman Emperor. A man of 'breeding', six foot seven inches tall, he inherited 6,000 acres of land in addition to his estate, and a couple of castles, Llanstephen and Amroth. In the twenties he claimed that his ships travelled 20 million miles annually, carried 15 million tons of cargo, $1\frac{1}{2}$ million passengers, and employed 36,000 men at sea and

23,000 on shore. It is little wonder that the Daily Post called him the 'Napoleon of Shipping' in its obituary in June 1937.

He started his romance with the shipping industry in 1902, when he helped to re-organise the Royal Mail Steam Packet Company and became the chairman. His list of acquisitions over the next twenty years reads like a compendium of Liverpool shipping lines; Pacific Steam Navigation; Lamport and Holt; Nelson Line; MacIver Line; Elder Dempster; Glen Line; Union Castle; Coast Lines; and Moss and Hutchinson. His professed aim was to replace J. Pierpoint Morgan as the biggest shipowner in the world. By the mid-thirties, he was the director of forty companies, including Harland and Wolf. A tycoon, even by today's standards. Yet the jewel that he wanted to add to his crown eluded him.

The White Star Line, with Cunard, controlled the blue riband of the shipping world – the passenger traffic on the North Atlantic. In the mid-nineteen-twenties Morgan, the director, was anxious to sell off the White Star interests, under the operating title of Ocean Steam Navigation Company. Furness Withy were interested, first in league with Cunard, but later alone. However, they pulled out when the figures showed that they were unlikely to get an eight per cent return. So, by 1926, the field was open for Kylsant and the Royal Mail Group, which was essentially a holding company of all the group's shipping interests. Such holding companies were a phenomenon of the international financial world of the nineteen-twenties. In order to buy the OSNC from Morgan for £7 million, Kylsant raised the capital by setting up a new company – White Star Lines Ltd – with a share capital of £9 million. However, by December 1931, this company was unable to meet its debts. Lord Kylsant, with rather ungentlemanly haste, fled to South Africa. He did eventually do the right thing, and returned to face the music. His trial, at the Old Bailey (admission by ticket only) revealed that he had issued 'false' prospectuses, to give the impression that Royal Mail had been trading at a profit, when it had not. Lord Kylsant was convicted, and spent ten months in prison. Not for him the stewardess's escape.

The Respectable Ruling Class
The source of the wealth of the Liverpool ruling class has not always, as in Lord Kylsant's case, been of dubious origins. Since the late nineteenth century, Liverpool has spawned countless millionaires, largely on

the basis of trade and commerce relating to the activity of the port. This was an era when shipowners, brokers and merchants like the Holts, Cunard, Brocklehurst, Harrison and Bowring amassed large fortunes. So, too, did the bankers, insurance dealers and financiers whose livelihoods were closely linked with the trading interests of the port. Often these interests overlapped. For example, the Holt family held interests in banking and cotton broking, shipping and the MDHC. Not surprisingly, these symbiotic economic interests created strong social and political bonds. Intermarriage, inter-locking boards of directors, vast networks of social activities, all led to the development of a powerful ruling class. Business was the unifying activity and as the adjoining chart shows, the wealth created survived well into the interwar period.

TABLE TWO
FAMOUS NAMES AND MONEY LEFT IN WILLS 1929-38

Year of Death	Name	Occupation	Money Left
1929	A. Hood	Cotton merchant	£500,000
	C. Lyle (Tates)	Sugar	£370,000
	J. Rankin	Gilmours – merchants	£800,000
	Sir Aubrey Brocklebank	Shipowner (Cunard)	£300,000
1930	T.H. Jackson	Great Western Railway Director	£660,000
	Major F. Bibby	Bibbys and GWR	£900,000
	Osbert Molyneux (Earl of Sefton)		£1,700,000
1931	G.H. Pilkington	Glass	£150,000
	R.M. Pilkington		£50,000
	Lord Melchett (Mond)	ICI	£1,'00,000
	A.B. Williamson	Balfour, Williamson	£600,000
1932	Sir A. Bicket	Shipowner	£200,000
	Lord Ferres	Merchant	£200,000
1933	J.D. Brunt	Sugar Broker	£230,000
	Sir J. Ellerman	Shipping	£17,230,000
1934	Sir Max Muspratt	ICI	£200,000
	T. Bickerton	Opthalmic Surgeon	£440,000
	Sir H. Harrison	Shipowner	£1,000,000
	Sir G.W. Paton	Bryant and May	£200,000
1936	Sir F.C. Bowring	Shipowner; Lloyds Insurance	£650,000
	R. Hooper	Cotton	£450,000
	F. Hornby	Meccano	£230,000

Year of Death	Name	Occupation	Money Left
1937	H. Brocklebank	Ship/post and Merchant	£870,000
	Lady Houston (Sir R.P.)	Shipowners	£1,500,000
	J. Choremi	Cotton	£1,100,000
	T. Jackson	Director	£700,000
1938	A. Earle	Corn Trader	£500,000
	J. Ismay	Shipowner (White Star)	£700,000
	E.B. Orme	MDHC and Martins Bank	£530,000

Politically, of course, this local ruling class remained divided between two major political philosophies – Liberalism and Toryism. On the whole those that were involved primarily in trade and commerce, like the Holts and the Rathbones, embraced Liberalism – constituting themselves as a 'Liberal plutocracy' within the local community – advocating free trade, low taxation and unitarianism. They sought to further these interests through active participation in local politics. Robert Holt had been the Liberal mayor of Liverpool in 1892. His son Lawrence took the same job in 1929. However, Liberalism in Liverpool never had either the support of a strong manufacturing 'elite' or the social basis (i.e. of a skilled working class) that it had elsewhere in the country. Consequently politics in Liverpool was dominated by traditional Toryism. The majority of the merchants and banking interests chose to put their weight behind the Tory Party as the most effective political way of securing their financial interests, particularly in the context of a city divided by sectarian rivalries (see Chapter 11). In this they had the support of the remnants of Liverpool's landed gentry. The large landowning families – the Seftons and the Derbys in particular – were eager not to be bypassed by economic developments. Motivated by a longstanding opposition to Liberalism and reform, they were well-integrated into the local Tory establishment.

Historically, then, the frontiers of the local political struggle had been drawn well before the first world war. Toryism, ruthlessly exploiting religious and economic divisions, maintained its hold in the face of an ever-weakening Liberal challenge and a growing Labour threat. But the situation was far from static. The economic restructuring that accompanied the interwar period had important implications for local 'worthies'. It was a period of continued realignment of forces within the ruling class. At the base of this realignment lay the two related historical trends that we have mentioned: the decline of liberalism and the growing incor-

Photos 21 & 22: Wealthy Liverpool residents exercising their horses around Sefton Park in January 1930. Little sign here of the effects of the Wall Street Crash a few months earlier.

poration of commercial and manufacturing interests into the Tory party. It is perhaps worth illustrating these two aspects in greater detail.

The Decline of Liberalism

Although Liberalism never achieved the electoral impact in Liverpool that it did nationally, it was, nevertheless, an important political force, particularly while the port flourished. But by the nineteen-twenties this was no longer the case. Shorn of economic power local Liberals like the Holts saw their political and social influence wane. The Holt family fortune was hard hit by taxation increases (by the nineteen-twenties a five-fold increase over the nineteen hundreds). Wealth is, of course, relative, and even in the mid-twenties Richard Holt was still able to maintain his large well-staffed houses in Liverpool, holiday homes in the Lake District and Wales, expensive sporting interests in golf, shooting and polo, and still had a few pence to pick up the odd Gainsborough. Yet even he was feeling the pinch. He was forced to sell his London house (63 Lowndes Square) in 1923 and had to cut down on his electioneering expenditure.

This economic decline was associated with a loss of social prestige and influence, a fact much lamented by Richard, who felt it to be symptomatic of a general decline in the quality of Liverpool's social elite. He bemoaned the closure, for economic reasons, of the highly fashionable Wellington Rooms – a popular meeting place for local 'high society'. He mused

"It is painful to think of this collapse of Liverpool society,and to reflect on what the place was thirty years ago."[2]

Politically, Richard became more remote from city politics. He was, he declared,

"horrified by the type of man chosen as Liberal candidate – mostly professionals – no one of any standing as far as I can judge."[3]

As leader of the Liverpool Liberal Federal Council, he felt the decline of liberal values in the face of socialistic developments particularly painfully.

"The more I see of socialistic developments – the less I like them. The stronger I feel in favour of leaving individuals the maximum of personal freedom including the right to make a thorough mess of their affairs."[4]

A political, as well as a social, snob, he opposed votes for women, rejected reforms and suggested that

"... The Liberal Party must concentrate their efforts on the outer districts and rally the better class of citizen against the Irish-Labour efforts to exploit the ratepayer – and the Tory dictatorship of Salvidge [Tory Leader]"[5]

Not surprisingly, given such leadership, the Liberals continued their decline throughout the interwar period until, in the words of one commentator,

"The Liverpool Liberal Party had become a conservative, class-based suburban rump, excluded from all vital areas of power and interest in the city."[6]

This decline might have been less pronounced had the Liberal Party been able to secure the support of the new manufacturing 'elite' which was becoming increasingly important in the industrial life of Liverpool. Our obituary list shows that alongside the well established manufacturers, like Bibby's and Tates, new names had emerged. Both large, like ICI, with Mond and Muspratt at the helm, and small, as Jacobs, Hornby [Mecanno] and Lyle all established themselves on Merseyside.

Initially, many of these manufacturers supported the Liberals. But their support was pragmatic and they increasingly defected to Tory ranks, preferring real political power to detached and lofty Liberalism. The career of Sir Max Muspratt is a good illustration of this. As head of I.C.I. and the Federation of British Industries, he was a radical free trader, and pursued an active career in Liberal politics. A councillor for Princes Park and Vauxhall, and Liberal leader after Bowring, he became mayor in 1916/17. However, by 1926 he had grown so disillusioned with the Liberals that he chose to cross the council floor. Eventually he took the chair of the Tory Finance committee and even emerged as a serious contender for the Tory leadership when Salvidge died in 1928.

A.E.Jacob and Sir Alfred Mond [later Lord Melchett] were other 'hard-headed businessmen' whose economic and political impulses led them to transfer their allegiance to the Tories. Such defections heralded the eclipse of the Liberal Party in Liverpool. The rise of Labourism was creating a polarisation in local politics and the ruling class responded by consolidating its power under the Tory banner.

Ruling Class Integration

The second major change during the inter-war period was in the social and economic composition of the Tory Party itself. Throughout the twenties and thirties, the Tories proved well able to accommodate a fusion of traditionally separated economic interests. In the first place, those involved in commerce and trade joined successfully with the bankers and merchants who had previously dominated the party. Many important commercial entrepreneurs put their support, and money, behind Tory electioneering. One such was Sir John Ellerman, the shipping magnate who had an empire stretching across Europe to the Far East, the Americas and the U.S.S.R. An interesting man, as his obituarist commented, "an individualist, a commercial giant, a money-maker of supreme ability". When he died in 1933, he left, according to his biographer, between £37 and £40 millions. Some backer! A valuable asset to any political party.

The Tories also proved able to incorporate the interests of the landed aristocracy. Vast areas of Liverpool were owned at this time by the Lords of Sefton and Derby. They adapted to the changing economic complexion of post World War One Liverpool with prudence. They sold land to the local authority (including 40,000 acres of Croxteth in Derby's case) and accrued great wealth from letting other property. In a city short of land theirs was an asset in great demand. In the course of amassing vast personal fortunes, these worthies took an increasing interest in local Tory politics. For them it seemed the best line of defence against the growing 'socialist menace'.

Some indication of the extent to which the ruling class became socially integrated during this period is evident in the social composition of those attending the funerals of any of Liverpool's great worthies of the time. The lists read like a Who's Who of the Liverpool ruling class; Bowrings; Seftons; Rathbones; Holts; Brocklehursts; Derbys; Lyles; and Rankins. United in death, if not in life.

But this alliance of economic interests needed to be translated into effective political action. The Liverpool Tory Party, ridden with sectarianism, and dominated by Salvidge and his idiosyncratic politics, needed some reform if it was to meet the demands being made upon it by its new sponsors. Interestingly, the responsibility for achieving this transformation fell upon the substantial shoulders of Edward George Villiers Stanley, seventeenth Earl of Derby – Lord Derby from 1908.

Lord Derby (1865-1948)

The 'chuckling Earl', 'Lancashire's chief asset', 'The father of Lancashire', 'an aristocrat of the old type', were just a few of the affectionate nicknames with which the man who dominated local politics for several decades was bestowed by an appreciative local press.

To put it mildly, Lord Derby was a very, very rich person. His estate netted £3,217,836. On his death, his horses, wines, cars, French properties, bonds and residences went to his wife. Most of the remainder found its way into Tory Party funds.

Elected M.P. for Westhoughton in 1892, he became Postmaster General in 1903 and soon emerged as an important national politician. He proved a fervent patriot, and in 1915, after the sinking of the *Lusitania*, with 1,198 deaths, he is reported to have said,

> "This country calls no longer for men to fight an honourable foe. It calls for men to hunt down a race of cold-blooded murderers."[7]

Not surprisingly, he was rewarded with the War Office ministry in 1916. However, it was in local politics that he proved most influential: as President of the Chamber of Commerce from 1910, Lord Mayor in 1911 and Freeman of the City in 1912. A local newspaper commented approvingly,

> "He carried out his duties with exemplary thoroughness and with the civic zest of a bourgeois blended with the aloof dignity of an aristocrat. As a figurehead and occasionally as peacemaker and constitution framer, he has taken an active part in the Conservative politics of the city. As president of the Chamber of Commerce for some years, he, from time to time, gave shrewd and valued advice to businessmen, and as chancellor of the University he has been a tower of strength."[8]

As one well able to appreciate the interlocking interests of business, inherited wealth and Toryism, it was natural that he should be invited to reorganise the local Tory party. For, under the autocratic leadership of Salvidge, the party had proved inflexible, sectarian and close to bankruptcy. Derby took over the Presidency of the Constitutional Association in 1928 and sought to achieve three main aims. First, he wanted to eliminate the influence of the Working Men's Conservative Association (W.M.C.A.) on Tory Policy, and to widen its electoral base. As he put it,

> "The W.M.C.A. as at present constituted is of no use. Half the men are socialists and we are relying on a broken reed when we think they could be of use to us."[9]

He preferred to gain the support of Catholic working class voters. Secondly, he sought to put the constituency parties on a sound footing financially, which meant attracting and cultivating support from local businessmen. Finally, he tried to separate parliamentary from municipal politics, by disconnecting ward and constituency associations. In short, this amounted to an attempt to give the party a greater *national* perspective.

Derby's intervention was resisted strongly by some sections of the Tory party. Nevertheless, although Derby did not fully achieve his aims, his endeavours were indicative of the growing awareness on the part of the local ruling class, of the need for a cohesive, united and efficient political party with a national perspective. If the inter-war period was not characterised by the emergence of a class-conscious proletariat locally, the same cannot be said of the ruling class.

However, it would be misleading to suggest that these developments amounted to a wholesale restructuring of class relations. Rather it represented a consolidation of existing historical trends. As Liberalism declined, the Tory party was able to fuse the, previously fragmented, commercial, landed and manufacturing elites into a major political force. This was hastened by the growing perception of a socialist threat. Lord Derby's intervention was important because it consolidated a national dimension. Local 'bossism', parochialism and sectarianism would no longer be allowed to prevent the achievement of electoral power. This was vital, given the fundamental national economic restructuring that was taking place throughout the inter-war period. In order to accommodate the national shift of financial interests to the South, the increasing rationalisation and transnationalisation of manufacturing production, and the threat to inherited wealth posed by the rise of socialism, the Liverpool ruling class had to close ranks – and it did.

Notes

1. Interview with Billy Weaver.
2. P.J. Waller, *Democracy and Sectarianism: A Political History of Liverpool 1868-1939* (Liverpool, University of Liverpool Press, 1981), pp.249-53.
3. Waller, p.278.
4. Waller, p.279.
5. Waller, p.279.
6. Waller, p.285.
7. *The Times*, 10.5.1915.
8. *Liverpool Metropolitan*, Nov. 1932.
9. Waller, p.321.

8
"ARE YOU WORKIN'?": DISCIPLINE AND SPEED UP

Mass unemployment affects not only those out of work – for whom the prospects of employment seem increasingly remote – but also those in work. A young woman in 1930 posed the question in these terms:

> I work in a wireless and electrical firm in Liverpool. We work a 47 hour week, and there are two shifts. If we are working days we get £1 a week, and for the night shift it's £1 2s 6d. Most of us are under 23 years of age and on the day shift there are many young workers who get as little as 8s a week. It is bitterly cold in the shop as the heating arrangements are bad and the ventilation is rotten. There are no canteens and we have to eat our meals on the benches in the workshops. The firm refuse to take anyone on in a union.
>
> We are getting well and truly rationalised on this job all right! Automatic processes have been put in which have put three out of every four workers out of work. One worker now has to look after four presses instead of one. We are all finding it hard to keep up with the new pace – but what can we do?[1]

This description of conditions of work was not novel for British industry sixty years ago. But the dramatic impact of increased exploitation of labour – now christened "productivity", and at the time called "speed-up" – was qualitatively different from what had gone before. "Rationalisation" was a favourite term in government and managerial circles. It heralded salvation for the nation, at the expense both of those who were sacked and for those who remained in the factories and workshops.

British industry and British capital was not in a good condition after the First World War. The financial and economic instability of companies and the nation was accentuated by international recession and, in 1929, by a crisis of credit. While those firms competing in the export markets – the staple industries of textiles, coal, and shipbuilding – were most severely affected, the crisis of over-production throughout the world economy had repercussions on all industries. Those so-called new industries that had a market in the British economy were not immune from intensified competition. What was the response to this crisis? How did firms respond to the sacrifices demanded on the altar of the market? And to what extent did Merseyside – with an economy based upon trade and distribution – suffer from the winds of change? Most importantly from our point of view, what did the nineteen-thirties mean for those who were in employment?

To re-establish profitability, production was re-organised to increase the exploitation of labour. It took different forms according to the nature of the work, the state of each economic sector, and the limits that collective organisation of workers could impose upon employers. But common throughout was the emphasis on rationalisation, a rather neutral sounding concept, but one with extremely decisive consequences. Speed-up, increased power of chargehands and supervisory staff, new technologies and an attack upon existing wages and conditions were all aspects of the employers' and state offensive in industry. But it required one extremely important accompaniment – the shackling of labour organisation. Some recent contributors to debates on industrial relations in the nineteen-twenties, have suggested that the decisive impact of those years was the "re-education of labour", both in the industrial and the political spheres.[2]

The employers offensive against the trade union movement was finally triumphant in the defeat of the general strike, and the starving back to work of the miners. This created a climate in which legislation was enacted that restricted trade unionism very tightly – like the Trades Dispute Act of 1927 which outlawed strikes designed to "coerce the government", initiated contracting in for Labour Party affiliation, made civil service union membership illegal and attacked mass picketing. Perhaps as important, the stage was set whereby collective organisation at work, to defend workers and to improve conditions, was ideologically threatened.

Threatened, but not smashed. Because hand in hand with restriction, went the co-option of trade union leaders into policy making. The Tory Minister of Labour after the general strike, Steel-Maitland, was convinced of the need for an "Industrial Concordat" of organised capital and organised labour. He was willingly supported by a section of British capital, especially those sections with interests in the domestic market. In 1928 and 1929, Sir Alfred Mond, Tory MP and chair of ICI led three conferences with the unions, partnered by Ben Turner from the Textile Workers' but spurred on by Ernest Bevin. At these meetings representatives of capital and labour discussed a whole series of questions, ranging from restrictive practices, to union amalgamations, and the gold standard. After 1926, many trade unions accepted willingly the invitation to participate in 'policy making', albeit not on their own terms, when it seemed that they were never to be consulted again. But such discussions and influence also demanded that those same trade union leaders conduct a war within the unions against those on the left who argued against this form of corporatism. Although the outcome of the so-called Mond-Turner talks never succeeded in influencing Tory government policy, it set the scene for trade union involvement, however passive, in the process of modernising, rationalising and reasserting managerial authority at work. All these were crucial in ensuring that rationalisation could be introduced without root-and-branch trade union opposition. It helped, after all, if your union had agreed to a "speed up".

The Bedaux System

In a climate of increasing unemployment and union demoralisation, it became relatively easy for managers to introduce new work practices and payment systems into industry, particularly in the manufacturing sector. One of the most popular and important was the Bedaux System. In theory this system, which centred on "time study",

> "... claimed to embrace a total approach to the questions of raising productivity and decreasing unit costs of production. It claimed to deal with the more efficient use of capital – factory layout, supplies of materials, adequate machinery and so on, as well as with the increased productivity as such."[3]

However, in practice the most important implication was the speeding-up of work and the increased exploitation of labour.

Under the Bedaux system, work was regarded as being made up of a series of movements and manipulations which required on the part of workers the expenditure of a certain amount of effort. These things, it was argued, could be measured and known accurately. The unit of measurement employed was called the 'B'. This represented the amount of work which could be performed by a worker in normal circumstances in one minute. The average worker, then, should have been able to get an output of sixty 'B's an hour – though Bedaux consultants regarded a standard of eighty 'B's as being attainable where workpeople and management were 100% efficient. 'Bs' produced beyond sixty an hour were called Premium 'Bs', for which a bonus was paid as incentive. The bonus for each premium 'B' was $\frac{1}{60}$th of the base rate of wage, and the Bedaux organisation recommended that $\frac{3}{4}$ of the bonus be paid to the workpeople directly concerned and the remaining quarter to supervisors and to indirect labour whose work had facilitated production in excess of the sixty 'Bs' standard.

Fundamentally the system was concerned with the establishment of supposedly "scientific" job timings to be implemented by strict supervision. It was a complex system but in essence it was aimed at increasing the intensity of work by making workers produce more during the working day for relatively less pay – an age-old management trick.[4]

If all this sounds rather complex and technical that should cause no great surprise. In the initial stages of Bedaux's introduction into plants bewilderment was one of the most common responses. There was, however, another reaction apart from bewilderment from the workforce. "Fed up" from BAT on Scotland Road wrote,

"The Bedaux speed-up system is now in operation here. Previously six girls worked on each table, now the work is being turned out by two. Whenever a girl leaves the room to go to the toilet or to get a drink – because of the heat and exhaustion – the Bedaux expert times them and if the next day it is found that they have not performed the right amount of work, they are reprimanded or sacked. So much more can be produced under this system that the firm are using short-time working, giving us one week off in four. Where will it end?"[5]

"Fed up" from BAT seemed to have had her question answered only two months later. At the 1932 Trades Union Congress in Newcastle, delegates overwhelmingly supported a clause in the General Council's report for the year which read:

"... such methods (the Bedaux system) have the effect, and in some cases, the intention of speeding up the individual worker to the greatest extent, regardless of his health, comfort and individuality. The object of such systems is to produce the maximum output per worker and carried to extremes, this has had very undesirable results both physiologically and psychologically. Overstrain and fatigue may follow and may, over a long period cause serious injury to the health of the worker. Moreover, the worker under such systems is made to feel that he is a cog in a machine for increasing output. The tendency is to obliterate individuality and craftsmanship and make the worker merely a machine."[6]

This is worth a brief comment. For over a hundred years before the Congress met in 1932, many people had argued that any worker in a capitalist framework was solely "a cog in a machine". Bedaux, and speed-up, only revealed the alienation in a more naked form. Secondly, the TUC construed it as an attack upon craft and male trade unionists – "his health", "he is a cog", "craftsmanship". In fact, it was mainly unorganised sections of the working class, and predominantly women workers, who suffered the stultifying and debilitating effects of the speed-up system and rationalisation. Lastly, the TUC were crying over their own spilt milk, because it was only possible to introduce such dramatic new work methods with the acceptance, if not open approval, of those delegates sitting in the conference hall. Occasionally, trade union branches had fought against Bedaux but after its introduction any reversal was extremely rare.

But who was Bedaux, who gave his name to the system, and to whom large sections of British manufacturing capital looked for salvation in the early thirties? Just another managerial whiz-kid with a missionary zeal? Yes, that, and yet something else – with an ingredient that gives a flavour of the political crisis of the thirties.

Charles Bedaux – A Man With a Mission

Bedaux was an interesting and little known character. He was born in 1886 in Paris, but emigrated to the U.S.A. in 1906. In the United States he took a variety of jobs selling life insurance and promoting a toothpaste which also removed inkspots! Eventually he worked for a Grand Rapids furniture company, and developed the system which was to make his fortune. In 1918 he founded the first Bedaux consultancy firm in Cleveland, and the success of his management system was such that he became the owner of two networks of Bedaux companies, one in the United States and one international, with offices from Chicago to Berlin to Bombay.

Bedaux and Fascism

In 1927, with a fortune in his pocket, Bedaux returned to France to live in luxury at his own chateau nears Tours. During the nineteen-thirties Bedaux moved more and more towards fascist politics, and became friendly with the Nazi elite, particularly Dr. Robert Ley, the Labour Front leader. The Duke of Windsor, after his abdication in 1936, was married at Bedaux's chateau, and Bedaux arranged a German tour for the ex-king. However, an attempted American tour for the Duke and Duchess of Windsor had to be cancelled, because Bedaux's support aroused a storm of protest from the American press and trade union leaders. For example, Francis Forman, President of the United Textile Workers, is quoted as saying "Mr Bedaux is a man who has made his money from the sweat and labour of the textile workers. I suggest he takes the Duke and Duchess on a tour of the southern textile districts to interview the men and women who are wandering around on relief as a result of his system". More important than the interrupted holiday plans of the Windsors was the fact that the fiasco of the cancelled tour led to an internal company revolt against Bedaux. Bedaux, close to breakdown, had to surrender control over his American company, though he retained 55% of the stock and control of Bedaux International. This defeat must have come as a shock to Bedaux, a person full of his own grandeur. As Janet Flanner put it, "Whatever type of modern management he may have counselled to his customers, his own was feudal, simple and single. He was it".[7] Nor was Bedaux's defeat confined to the U.S.A. The British Bedaux office followed the American palace revolt, and insisted on instituting a directorate, who, they thought, could run the British business with less publicity and suggestions of fascism. Bedaux retreated to his French chateau, and after the fall of France in 1940, became an industrial advisor to both the Nazis and the Vichy government. Bedaux had always had a strong sense of himself as engaged on a mission. Such was his profound belief in his system that he thought that production organised by his methods could do away with poverty. Moreover, he believed that an efficient society could come only from a revolution on the right, led by engineers and technocrats. It was his humanitarian duty, as an inspired systematizer, to build society up on a new technical basis. It was these views that made Bedaux welcome the Nazis as a new European elite. He was captured in North Africa in 1942 and put on trial for his war crimes in the States in 1944.[8]

There is no monument to those working people in Britain who directly suffered, either at work or as a result of unemployment at the hands of Bedaux. The border-line between fascism and autocratic management is occasionally very fine.

Discipline and Speed Up
People do not willingly sweat blood, even for the sake of a few extra pennies in times of hardship. They are compelled. With increasing frequency in the thirties, companies brought in tougher first line management. Michael Edwardes at British Leyland in the nineteen-eighties was not the first to enunciate the virtues of shop-floor discipline. Now was the time to bite your lip, keep in with the foreman and remember that dole queue just outside the gate. Arthur Exell, an exile from the Welsh valleys in the new car plants at Oxford, explains:

"Some of the foremen were brutal. I think Kendrick (the boss) liked that sort, he would find out who was the most horrid and give them the job. We had a terrible foreman who couldn't read or write ... but he was the foreman, and he would really drive you, he was on your tail you might say, following you all the time, making sure you kept working."[9]

It was again, not just a method employed against male workers.

"The 'Peckswear' clothing factory employs about 400 girls and has speeded up all the girls on the machines. They manufacture aprons and white coats for stewards, hairdressers and shop assistants. The girls are now compelled to turn out one dozen aprons in an hour instead of the usual time taken of two and a half hours. The foreman is now trying to make the girls do one dozen in forty minutes. The girls have to sew seven coats in seven different colours per hour and no time is allowed for the working of hard material, such as the difference between white and grey twill. Two girls have been dismissed for 'playing' in the dinner hour, and another was dismissed because she could not do her dozen in forty minutes and told the boss it could not be done."[10]

Speed up demanded greater discipline, not only at work but throughout the length of the working day, when on company premises. Any attempt to challenge instructions, to answer back or disagree meant the sack.

Such realities were not confined to factory life. In 1930, Woolworth's cafe in Church Street got a new supervisor. Her first act was to dismiss half the waitresses and demand that the others work twice as hard. One woman stuck at it for six days and then left. The pace was too much. When applying for unemployment benefit, she was put on stop for three weeks and had her case referred to the Court of Referees. They upheld the supervisor's actions by deeming her to have voluntarily left employment, and so disqualifying herself from eligibility to benefit.[11]

"As Many Legs as a Centipede ..."; New Technology

Forms of intensification of work and increased managerial control were extensions, albeit very radical extensions, of existing methods of production and supervision. But another aspect of the rationalisation of British capital in the thirties was very new. Faced with the slump consequent upon massive overproduction, some firms were in a position to reorganise production totally. In the last ten years in Britain, the phrase 'new technology' has been used to disguise or camouflage the creation of unemployment; but in the thirties, pressures to be competitive produced a similar response.

Tate & Lyle's sugar refinery in Love Lane underwent total re-equipping in the thirties. In the whole history of the plant until the 1980 closure, the most dramatic strides made in boosting productivity were achieved in the thirties. Across the Mersey at Port Sunlight, Lever Brothers initiated a parallel series of "internal reorganisations" – that ubiquitous phrase, so loved by official company historians. But perhaps the most dramatic examples of the implication and effect of new machinery and increased labour productivity, was on the waterfront. As ever, the labour intensive nature of work in the port – which had been favoured by port employers given the massive pool of labour available – meant dockworkers were in the forefront of rationalisation.

In 1930, a docker working on the Gladstone Dock – one of the latest developments by the Mersey Dock and Harbour Board – wrote about the,

"... new machines, electrical cranes, belt conveyors, grain elevators and coal tips that have been installed along the fourteen miles of the Liverpool docks which has directly led to the displacement of dockers."[12]

More particularly, he cited the new practices at his dock where, subsequent to the introduction of "overhead cranes and electrical trucks", the employers were deliberately violating the Port Working Rule Book by increasing the number of bags in a sling and decreasing the number of men in a gang. Just over a year later, the same correspondent to the *Daily Worker* reported on the harassment of dockers at the daily stand by the police and continued:

"At the Gladstone Dock three-legged and four-legged cranes have been introduced. In the near future, these cranes may have as many legs as a centipede. The three-legged crane displaces 34 dockers and divides their wages between the Dock Board and the shipowners ... When this displacement of men was brought to the notice of No. 12 branch of the union (TGWU), they said they knew nothing about it."[13]

Two months later, William Railston, a TGWU member from the docks, was telling a conference in London of a new coal elevator on the dock.

"... this elevator displaces a lot of men, about 20 or 30, and will unload coal ships at 500 tons an hour. The shipowners get richer and richer, the stevedores and the dockers are forced to submit."[14]

By 1934, new machinery and 'displacement' had reached the Huskisson Dock. The dockers were out for ten days in protest against the operation of a new sugar conveyor which offloaded so quickly that dockers were in danger of getting buried. But now the effects of rationalisation were becoming apparent. Output per docker had risen by nearly one-quarter in the previous ten years, and in 1934, there were more accidents reported in the first three months of the year than in the whole of the preceding year. New technology was taking its toll. Changes provoked many disputes. Some reached the pages of the local press, most did not. What provoked opposition was not only the direct unemployment resulting from the electrical cranes, the elevators, and the pumps, but also the effects this had upon existing work practices. Management used new machinery as an ideal opportunity to break established agreements and port working rules. The displacement of dockers, and the erosion of numbers in a gang had severe consequences for those who remained, not least in terms of health and safety.

The Assault on Wages and Conditions

For those in work, the thirties had benefits we are told. Real wages rose. But what about the conditions under which people worked? How long did people have to work to preserve existing living standards, and even their jobs? In 1929, the Liverpool branch of the Union of Postal Workers held a protest meeting against the addition of three hours work per day for women telephonists. Five years later the papers carried a story of "several telephonists being admitted to hospital suffering from exhaustion after being forced to work from 7am to 11pm" – a sixteen hour day![15]

In 1930, all but one of the twelve cinemas in Liverpool were closed through a strike by projectionists, members of the Electrical Trades Union. They argued that the introduction of "talkies" had demanded rehearsals and placed a severe strain on the operators. A sixty hour week was commonplace. The whip of the dole queue forced workers to knuckle under. Longer hours were prevalent.

Accidents resulted, and people's health was jeopardised. In some instances, death was the consequence of employers' demands. On 29th July 1932, the *Daily Post* carried a short story of a conductor on the trams who had been killed whilst running from his bus to snatch a cup of tea. Both the management and the union responded by outlawing tea breaks while on duty! The causes of such tragic events were not examined at the time. Nine months had to elapse before an analysis of the Liverpool tramways was forthcoming. All the manoeuvres of a classical nineteen-thirties employer – a Tory Council – are evident in the tramways service. We reprint in full the resolution passed by the TGWU Tramway Workers in March 1933 which speaks so eloquently for itself and illustrates management strategy. The public sector in the thirties was not immune from the sweep of rationalisation.

"RESOLUTION PASSED BY A MASS MEETING OF LIVERPOOL TRAMWAY WORKERS & TGWU.

The Walton branch of the Transport and General Workers Union, together with the representatives from Edge Lane, Green Lane and Litherland branches of Tramways and Busmen, call attention to the fact that the net profit of £120,000 was shown by the Tramways Undertaking for the year ending March 1932, and a net profit of £119,000 for the year ending March 1933.

This is in spite of the fact that rides to the value of £45,000 are granted free by the City Council and in addition, to paying interest and making provision for sinking funds to the extent of £136,000 a year.

We do not in any way criticise the provisions made for disabled men, the blind or aged. But we do in the most emphatic way protest against the Tramways Committee policy of putting the burden upon the employees of the Department by mass dismissals, speeding up, short time working and a general lowering of the already low standards, all on the plea of the alleged financial embarrassment of the undertaking.

We claim that the alleged redundancy, which has led to many dismissals, has been created by the carrying through of a policy which involved:

a) the failure of the Tramway Committee to set up training schools for busmen
b) reduction in time allowed for signing on from 15 minutes to ten minutes.
c) introduction of excessively long spread-over duties with the need for fewer men
d) speeding-up of journeys involving, in some cases, a full tour of duty without a single minute for food or other natural purposes!
e) the posting of duties exceeding 8 hours by as much as 30 and 40 minutes – despite the existence of an agreement stating that "the working week shall consist of six days of eight hours per day"; resulting in an increased mileage with fewer men.
f) increasing the weekly hours of work at flat rate from 48 hours to 51 hours per week.

All these measures are part and parcel of one fixed policy – to create an artificial redundancy and then to use that redundancy to smash even bad agreements, and to lower conditions to a degree which would not have been possible under other circumstances. Men with years of service are denied a regular guaranteed wage; men stand by at their depots for hours before getting a day's work, without being paid for waiting time.

In the sheds, men are doing semi-skilled work for labourers' pay; gangs of cleaners depleted to half the normal strength, are expected to maintain average output; lads approaching the age of 21 may be dismissed after years of service before they become entitled to an adult wage.

Men are thrown carelessly onto the streets in a city where already 100,000 people vainly look for a job. And side by side with this, men already working a 48 hour week, are asked to work overtime at ordinary rates because there is a shortage of men!

In the face of these conditions, we demand that dismissals shall cease; we say that given decent working conditions equivalent to those of any comparable town, not only would dismissals be unnecessary, but that those men who have already been dismissed, could be absorbed.

We claim the right as municipal servants to satisfactory conditions absolutely, irrespective of financial situations for which we have no responsibility.

We therefore instruct our officials to give this protest the widest possible publicity through the press, both local and national, in order that the pressure of public opinion may be exercised on those responsible."[16]

It was not sufficient to "instruct our officials to give this protest the widest possible publicity". There was another union with a larger membership in the tramways department that was recognised by the Tramways Committee. In April 1933 the two local officials of the National Union of General and Municipal Workers signed a new agreement. They went on record as saying that "the agreement with the Liverpool Corporation is the finest in the transport industry in the country".[17] This view was not shared by other people including some tramway workers. The agreement was signed behind locked doors in the Picton Hall and a police guard was required by the negotiators upon emerging!

The effect of the depression on people in work is often ignored but for trade unionists it was the most immediate consequence of mass unemployment. Tragically the scenes outside the Picton Hall were all too common and attempts to maintain wages and conditions lacked the necessary enthusiasm at official level. This revealed the limitations of trade unionism and the absence of a coherent political direction within the labour movement.

Notes
1. *Daily Worker*, 4.1.30.
2. See, for example, K. Burgess, *The Challenge of Labour* (London, Croom Helm, 1980).
3. G. Brown, *Sabotage* (Nottingham, Spokesman Books, 1977), p.232.
4. Brown, *Sabotage*, p.233.
5. *Daily Worker*, 29.7.32.
6. *T.U.C. Report* 1933.
7. New Yorker, 22.9.1945, p.29.
8. C. Littler, *The Development of the Labour Process in Capitalist Society* (London, Heinemann, 1982).

9. A. Exell, 'Morris Motors in the 1930s – Pt.I', *History Workshop*, No.6, Autumn 1978, p.53.
10. *Daily Worker*, 25.4.31.
11. *Daily Worker*, 15.5.30.
12. *Daily Worker*, 11.1.30.
13. *Daily Worker*, 14.2.31.
14. *Daily Worker*, 13.4.31.
15. *Liverpool Daily Post*, 9.7.1929.
16. *Daily Worker*, 31.3.1933.
17. *Daily Worker*, 12.4.33.

PART THREE
THE FIGHT BACK?

9
THE LONG HAUL: TRADE UNIONS ON MERSEYSIDE

In the context of mass unemployment in the inter-war period, trade unions were fighting to survive in a hostile environment. The gains made before 1914 and the years immediately after 1918 were hard to sustain when there were never fewer than one million unemployed from the early twenties right through to 1939. As soon as unemployment began to rise in 1920, the membership of the trade union movement began to fall. From a peak of over 8 million in 1920, there was a more or less steady fall in numbers to a low point of just over 4 million in 1933. So the thirties saw trade unionism starting at a low ebb in terms of membership and financial strength.

However, it was also significant that the biggest losses were concentrated in those areas where organisation had previously been strongest.

Photo 23: August 1911, Liverpool Transport Strike, the crowd at St. George's Plateau. Smiling faces, and ultimately a great victory for trade unions on Merseyside, but two decades later in the thirties the movement was on the defensive.

The depression hit the basic staple industries of the British economy hardest – iron and steel, textiles and coal in particular – and it was in these industries that the centre of trade unionism had been based. As they declined, other industries became relatively more important – the service industries, the distributive trades, transport and the "new" industries like motor cars, household appliances and other consumer goods. This structural shift had a number of profound implications for the trade union movement.

First, the new areas of importance were ones that had traditionally been less well organised in terms of unionisation. Second, many new factories and even whole industries, for example, the motor industry, had to be organised from scratch. Third, the nature of the labour force in these industries was different, with a far higher proportion of workers classified as unskilled or semi-skilled. Fourth, the geographical structure of the labour force was changing – the old emphasis on the north of England, Wales and Scotland was shifting towards the West Midlands, London and the South-East, while industry was also beginning to move away from the old city centres to new estates on the periphery of towns. Fifth, the gender structure of the labour force was also changing. With the notable exception of textiles, the old staple industries had been to a very great extent male industries, whereas in the new areas of growth there was generally a much higher proportion of women workers involved.

The trade union movement then was faced with a challenge to its old structures and practises in the thirties, a challenge which was faced up to only slowly and with a limited degree of success. The twenties had been a decade in which the unions were primarily concerned with defending their members in the old staple industries against wage cuts and job losses, often through large-scale, national strikes. The General Strike of 1926 represented the culmination and also the crucial defeat of these tactics. In contrast, throughout the thirties there was only one major strike in defence of workers in an old staple industry – the More Looms dispute in the Lancashire textile districts in 1932. The emphasis shifted to smaller-scale, more localised activities, mainly concerned with organising new industries, or previously poorly organised industries. Disputes generally were of short duration, and tended to involve relatively small numbers of workers.

133

To some extent these new tactics did meet with some success. Local victories over union recognition were won and some new industries were organised successfully. From 1933 union membership began to rise again, passing the six million mark by 1938, and to a great extent these new members were recruited in new areas. Thus the unions that sustained the largest growth in the thirties were the Transport & General and the General & Municipal, both general unions of major importance in service, distribution, transport and the "new" industries. This shift is reflected in the fact that unions representing miners, engineering workers, weavers and boilermakers between them made up 26.2% of TUC membership in 1930, but only 22.7% by 1938.[1] On the other hand, the T & G, G & M, Shop Assistants Union and the National Union of Distributive and Allied Workers between them accounted for 21.5% of TUC membership in 1930, rising to 28% by 1938.[2]

However, change was still too slow in response to changing circumstances. By 1936 only 31% of the total labour force had been unionised. Many of the "new" industries were only partially organised, and some not at all. By the mid-thirties, for example, only the most "skilled" sections of the motor industry had been unionised, and despite some gains the distributive and service industries were still poorly organised by the end of the decade. Perhaps 10% unionised in the distributive trades by 1939 would not be an overestimate.

Moreover, the trade union movement was still to a large extent a male dominated movement. More women did join unions in the thirties, but still only 16% of all women in paid employment were unionised by the late thirties, compared with almost 40% of men.[3] Women still only made up 15% of total union membership, although they made up over 30% of the total paid workforce in Britain. As for the leadership of unions, even in those with a large proportion of women workers the leaders were predominantly men. For instance, the Amalgamated Weavers Association, by far the largest union with a predominantly female membership – in 1926 women made up about three-quarters of the total membership of 160,000 – sent only two women in a total delegation of forty-seven to the 1927 TUC Conference. Ten years later membership of the union had fallen dramatically to 90,000, with four-fifths now women workers, and yet at the conference of 1937 there were still only three women delegates out of at total of forty-four.[4] This massive imbalance was reflected throughout the movement, and showed little change in the thirties despite the structural shifts taking place in the workforce. In 1925 there were only eighteen women delegates at the TUC conference out of a total of 727; by the 1936 conference women delegates had actually fallen to twelve out of a total of 603.[5]

Photo 24: The Match-Girls' Strike, Bryant & May's, London, 1888. An early attempt at unionising women, but by the thirties the trade union movement had still only organised a small proportion of women workers.

At another level the union movement was also weak in the thirties in terms of its overall political strategy. Up to 1926, many trade unionists saw the crisis of the British economy in terms of the failure of the capitalist system, and the response to that failure took the form of militant working class action. Thus union leaders, sometimes reluctantly, were forced into major industrial battles with employers to fight wage cuts and loss of jobs. With the failure of the General Strike in 1926, and the consequent Trades Disputes Act which limited the powers of trade unions, the strategy of the Trade Union Movement as a whole changed drastically. The demoralisation of the rank and file allowed the leadership to move towards a policy of consultation with employers over the rationalisation of industry, and increasing conciliation and arbitration at a national level, seen most clearly in the Mond-Turner talks in 1928. These talks set the tone for TUC strategy throughout the thirties. Co-operation within the capitalist system replaced confrontation with capital.

There was opposition to this strategy, particularly by the Communist led National Minority Movement among the rank and file. But increasingly this opposition was crushed by the TUC and the leadership of the major unions. Witch hunts against Communists and CP sympathisers were pursued in the unions throughout the thirties, serving to isolate and demoralise opposition. The leading figures of the movement in the thirties became Ernest Bevin, leader of the T&G and a relentless anti-communist, and Walter Citrine, secretary of the TUC and a moderate who never tired of preaching the benefits of co-operation with employers. Citrine's strategy was summed up in his claim that the unions were the "labour side of management".

The crucial failure of the trade union movement in the thirties was in combating the twin attack of mass unemployment and rationalisation. As we show in Chapter 12, the unions were reluctant to do anything positive to organise the unemployed. Their priority lay with their members who managed to hang on to their jobs, and their attitude to the National Unemployed Workers Movement (NUWM) from 1926 was that it was a Communist front that should be kept at arms length. When the TUC did begin to set up Unemployed Associations from 1933 it was purely as a defensive response to the growing influence of the NUWM among the unemployed and even among union members in work. As a consequence, these associations were unable to organise the unemployed in any meaningful sense, and failed miserably, most eventually merging into the NUWM. Their failure has been described by two historians of the TUC thus:

"The Associations did not prove a success. Their activities were narrowly defined, and the anxiety to keep them under control was evident from the beginning ... Too much emphasis was placed on the Associations as a source of future union recruitment ... the reasons for their formation were essentially negative, reflecting the narrow self-interest of industrial unions, and the ideological antagonisms of the TUC leadership to Communist militancy."[6]

The response to rationalisation was equally unsuccessful, as we demonstrated in Chapter 8. Ultimately it was often the union official as much as the foreman who was seen as the "enemy" in these circumstances.

Thus in the nineteen-thirties the Trade Union movement was moderate in its policies, monolithic in its structures. Faced with mass unemployment, falling membership, rationalisation and a changing economic base, it adopted a conciliatory, cautious response. Any attempt to mount a militant attack against the failures of the economic system was stifled by the official leadership and was forced to take an "unofficial" character. The rank and file busmen's movement in London was the best known and also the most successful example of this "unofficial" unionism. By 1937 this movement had forced the T&GWU leadership into an official strike in London, accompanied by unofficial action in the provinces – but the strike eventually failed, and Ernest Bevin was able to break the movement. Trade unionism was basically unable to protect or advance the interests of the working class in the "low, dishonest decade" of the thirties.

The only glimmer of hope in the Trade Union movement was to be found at a local level. There were local struggles to unionise factories and workshops, often involving workforces new to the very idea of unionism. This involved small scale struggles against wage-cuts, job-losses and speed-ups, often in opposition to local or national union leadership, and struggles within unions to democratise their structures and practises, in order to curb the power of autocratic leaders. These were the most positive features of trade unionism in the thirties. It was mostly a long, hard and unglamorous struggle which never hit the headlines in the way that the big strikes of the twenties did. Nevertheless, the struggle went on.

Photos 25, 26 & 27: Scenes from one of the few major strikes of the thirties — the dispute over wage cuts and speed-up in the cotton textile districts in 1932. (25) Above: Strikers at Blackburn, (26) Right: pickets in Preston, and (27) Opposite: workers returning to work in Preston, smiling and defiant despite having been beaten.

Photo 27

The Local Scene

"Most of the union officials that I knew had been dockers, and in some cases they'd been really militant men, and it appeared to me that the more militant you were the sooner you got a job as a delegate, and then you seemed to lose all track. There were times when you could send for a delegate over a boat, or something that had gone wrong and he'd side with the boss! He'd say 'Oh, come on boys, it's only this one ... come on boys'. Where did you go from there? You couldn't win. All you could do was call him, but he didn't care what you called him, he was a paid official and he was there for life. He lived the life of Riley. Trying to get them out of their little offices was murder – you'd get a feller out of Walton gaol quicker. This is the thing, your delegates let you down."[7]

In many ways the problems of Trade Unions on Merseyside were the same in the thirties as they had always been. The most important sectors of employment in the area had been in transport, distribution, service industries and small workshop production. So the structural shift in the national economy that took place in the thirties only tended to make Merseyside appear less atypical of the national picture than it had been earlier. The focus of trade unionism locally continued to be the struggle to organise workers traditionally classified as unskilled or semi-skilled, often casually employed, mainly into general rather than craft unions. This involved organising the docks, the ships, small factories or workshops, all areas that had always been hardest to unionise. Moreover, the nature of much work on the dockside meant that local bargaining over conditions and work practices had always been common – rationalisation was only an extra pressure on top of the continual struggle over the degree of control over work. The emphasis was on unofficial disputes, local bargaining on wages and conditions, small scale actions to gain union recognition.

The conflict between autocratic leaders and rank and file militants was nothing new to Merseyside in the thirties either. The dominance of right wing leaders like Bevin and Citrine in the union movement of the thirties would have been familiar to union activists in Liverpool used to the earlier dominance of figures like Havelock Wilson in the Seamen's Union and Jimmy Sexton in the Dockers' Union. We can get an idea of some local rank and file attitudes to union officials on the docks from an article by a docker in the *Daily Worker* in 1931:

"ISSUES IN THE LIVERPOOL DOCKS: UNION DELEGATES WHO DO NOTHING
– by a Liverpool docker.

There are many issues today which concern the Liverpool docker. One is the very shabby way in which he is oftimes treated by the officials and delegates of his union.

Oftimes members of the Union fall into arrears through no fault of their own, they seek work, but it does not materialise. Hence they are unable to earn enough to subsist on, and cannot afford the humble tanner which is needed towards their 'quarterly badge".

The day dawns on which they are lucky and the foreman pulls him out of the stand but the eagle eye of the delegate is on him and he queries him with "where's your button? Oh this won't do! Why this is last quarter's badge. Go and get it, then you'll get a job". All right for the delegate who has a good week's wage, a well filled stomach and a good home to walk into...

One truly wonders at the manners of the union delegates; they don't seem to care about the dockers, only their own good wages, and to keep their avaricious eyes upon their sinecures – for as a rule when they are elected they seem to take root in the foundations of the branch offices.

Where are the delegates when the men are being rushed and bullied, when there are men short in gangs – which means the overworked dockers having to pull out for another man's work who is not on?

Then when there are overloaded trucks, overloaded bogies, too much cargo in slings by far too much, the delegates are not there then; oh dear no!

If you mention anything: "Oh, I spoke to the boss and I can't help it". This is the "justice" which is dealt out by the delegates of the Dockers' Union."[8]

So there were no big industrial disputes on Merseyside in the thirties, but rather a series of tactical skirmishes. On the dockside, typical examples were the week-long stoppage by dockers at the Princes Dock in June/July 1933 in support of Irish seamen on the Liverpool to Ireland cargo routes, who were attempting to resist wage cuts; and the dispute in September 1934 at the Birkenhead docks when dockers refused to work overtime as an attempt to share out scarce work among the union membership.[9] Both of these disputes ended in defeat, and significantly in both cases the official union line was to oppose the action. The NUS tried desperately to persuade the dockers not to strike over the Irish boats in 1933, and the Irish seamen involved left the NUS and formed their own union due to the refusal of the NUS officials to support their claims. In Birkenhead in 1934 the Union official argued from the beginning that the overtime ban should not be supported. The official concerned, McVey, was continually echoing the arguments of the management of the Clan Line, and later the Blue Funnel line, who threatened to move their trade away from Birkenhead across the river to Liverpool docks unless the Birkenhead men gave in. With the union offering little support, perhaps it is understandable that the dockers conceded in the end – but the constant, hidden battle that went on the docks is shown by the fact that two weeks after the dispute, while working the overtime, they were doing their best to slow down the work on the Clan Line boats by adopting "ca'canny" methods.[10]

Outside the dock gates, it was a similar picture of small-scale disputes over wages and conditions – by slaughterers at Stanley Cattle Market in May 1933 over wage reductions, which was won; by workers at the British Enka Artificial silk works in Aintree over wage cuts in December 1934, also won; by glass cutters at Pilkingtons in St. Helens in November 1933 over the imposition of the Bedaux system; by workers at Walkers Dairies in February 1934 and at Howard, Ford & Co., Woolton in July 1935 over attempts by management to restrict the activities of the union (NUDAW and NUGMW respectively).[11]

The most successful aspect of union activity in this period, however, was in unionising areas that had been previously unorganised. Unions like NUDAW, NUGMW, T&GWU, Shop Assistants Union and the Tailors and Garment Workers Union did succeed in unionising various small shops, warehouses, workshops and factories on Merseyside in the thirties.

The best documented example of this activity is the tailoring trade. In 1933 the Tailors and Garment Workers Union succeeded in gaining recognition at Burtons' tailoring workshop in Liverpool. Following this success the union made concerted efforts to organise workers in other workshops, and a crucial battle ensued at the Donegal Tweed Co. This was a small tailoring workshop situated on Fleet Street in Liverpool city centre, and typical of its kind. It employed 150 workers, predominantly young and with a high proportion of women workers. It had long been known as a non-union shop, and all previous attempts to unionise it had been unsuccessful.

In February 1934, following the successful unionisation of Burton's, new attempts were made to establish a union at Donegal Tweed. A factory committee was set up and a group of the workers joined the Tailors and Garment Workers Union. Over the next few months this group held various meetings and also organised other workshops. They attempted to set up a youth section of the Union, and sent a resolution to Liverpool Trades Council asking for support. The Trades Council was anything but encouraging, with some delegates from other unions reportedly greeting the resolution with "sneers".

Nevertheless, the members at Donegal Tweed continued to fight for a union in the shop. In July 1934 they organised a social in the evening for young workers. The following morning (5th July) the management of the firm called one of the workers who had attended the social into the office and asked him to list the names of all those employees who had attended, and also to explain what had taken place at the social. The worker refused, and was promptly sacked.

At noon that day the cutting department walked out in support of the sacked youth, followed by the rest of the workforce later in the day. A strike committee was elected, and a set of demands were drawn up for presentation to the management. For the next two days pickets were mounted, and despite a strong police presence, all attempts by management to bring in scab labour were foiled.

In the face of this unexpected militancy by the workforce, on the third day of the strike the management backed down completely. They agreed to meet the strike committee and conceded the following demands: full reinstatement of the strikers; full recognition of the union in the factory; increases in the rates of pay on some jobs; twelve hours notice of overtime to be given to workers in future; punctual payment of wages; and other minor concessions on working conditions. The strike had been a total victory for the workforce, and after the settlement the entire workforce joined the Tailors and Garment Workers Union.[12]

The sequel to this dispute was a steady growth of the union in other workshops in Liverpool in the next few years. In 1935 a local official was asked to address a meeting of tailoring workers in London who were trying to spread the union in the metropolis, so successful were the tactics of the union on Merseyside seen in the rest of the country.

We have concentrated on the Donegal Tweed dispute because it illustrates key features of trade unionism in the thirties. First, the nature of disputes in the decade – small, localised, and of short duration. Secondly, that real successes were possible in the thirties, in an industry well known for poor working conditions and being difficult to unionise. Victories could be won by determined action. The thirties may have been generally a decade of defensive rearguard actions by the unions, and the stirring days of mass action like the General Strike were not repeated, but at a local level it didn't always appear a picture of gloom and retreat.

Notes
1. N. Branson & M. Heinemann, *Britain in the Nineteen Thirties* (London, Weidenfeld & Nicolson, 1971), p.371.
2. Branson & Heinemann, p.371
3. Branson & Heinemann, pp.148-9.
4. T.U.C., *Annual Reports*, 1927 and 1937.
5. N.C. Soldon, *Women in British Trade Unions 1874-1976* (Dublin, Gill & Macmillan, 1978), p.122.
6. J. Lovell and B.C. Roberts, *A Short History of the TUC* (London, Macmillan, 1968), p.129.
7. Interview with George Hughes.
8. *Daily Worker*, 31.1.1931.
9. *Liverpool Daily Post*, 29.6.1933-6.7.1933; 18.9.1934-25.9.1934.
10. *Liverpool Daily Post*, 8.10.1934.
11. *Liverpool Daily Post*, 15.5.1933; 8.12.34; 6.11.33; 9.2.34; 25.7.35.
12. *Daily Worker*, 7.7.1934 and 10.7.1934; *Liverpool Daily Post*, 6.7.1934.

10
LABOUR AND THE SLUMP: THE LIVERPOOL LABOUR PARTY

One month after the Wall Street crash in 1929, the Liverpool Labour Party achieved an historic victory. It received little mention at the time – essentially because it was regarded by friend and foe as being inevitable. A Labour Government was in office in London and events in Liverpool only seemed to indicate the vibrancy of the Party throughout the country. The historic victory was the success of the Liverpool Labour Party in winning over one-half of the vote at the November council elections. As only one quarter of the council were standing for election, this electoral success did not mean the arrival of a Labour controlled City Council. Was this, however, the opening response of Liverpool's working class to the dramatic events that had just been reported in the United States' financial nerve centre? Did this electoral supremacy reflect the willingness of the local working class to confront capitalist instability? More crucially, what did the local election results of 1929 mean in the wider context of the Labour Party's response to mass unemployment?

The 1929 Labour Government

The manifesto on which the Labour Party fought the general election of 1929 contained few radical proposals. Much was promised – but little of a socialist nature. The tackling of unemployment was made explicit as being the cardinal point of government policy. Indeed the manifesto carried an "unqualified pledge" to that effect, coupled with the need to improve the lot of the unemployed. Once in power, the Labour Cabinet's acceptance of Treasury advice concerning balanced budgets precluded any radical attack on the growing economic crisis. When Labour took office, unemployment stood at just over one million. By the summer of 1931 almost three times as many people were out of work. Claims that the government's enthusiasm was tempered by its minority position in the House of Commons and the need to forge an alliance with the Liberals were irrelevant. The rise in unemployment only provoked a crisis when it increased the debt of the Unemployment Insurance Fund. The burden of transitional benefits on the budget, at a time when government revenues from taxation were falling, meant that the Budget would not balance. By the time the May Committee's report was brought to the

Cabinet in July 1931, demanding savage cuts in public spending, Labour opposition was futile; after all this was the logical conclusion of their own policy for the previous two years.

The May Committee demanded an immediate 20% reduction in unemployment benefit and equivalent wage reductions for public sector workers. Some of the Labour Cabinet could not take the final step which would so clearly abandon their claims to represent the working class. Ramsey MacDonald, Philip Snowden and J.H. Thomas had no such qualms and the Labour Cabinet was irrevocably split. Finally, these three crossed the floor of the House and formed a National Government in alliance with Tories and Liberals. At the subsequent general election of October 1931, they claimed a mandate for the implementation of the cuts. Labour lost $1^1/_2$ million disillusioned supporters, and its Parliamentary strength fell from 288 seats to only fifty-two. Against the backcloth of three million people unemployed, what did this mean for the British Labour Party?

One historian, John Saville, has emphasised three interwoven themes that grew in dominance after 1926, and certainly after the electoral defeat in 1931.[1] First, it is argued, the only possible road was the road of Parliamentary democracy. Although by no means a novel component of the Labour ideology, now every campaign and policy was to be carefully scrutinised as to its eventual effectiveness in securing a majority in the 'seat of democracy'. This meant, to an overwhelming extent, that the Labour Party waged no major campaign over any of the numerous issues that faced the working class in the decade.

Secondly, the Labour Party was to distance itself from any association with the Communist Party and any campaign which it considered tainted with Communist influence. It was carefully guided in this by Ernest Bevin and Walter Citrine in the General Council of the TUC who became increasingly effective practitioners in the art of recognising "disruptive elements" and "red policies". For the Labour Party association with the Communist Party was seen both as a vote loser, and as a threat to its exclusive focus on the Parliamentary road.

Lastly, internal debate was stamped on. Such democracy as did exist within the Party structure was consistently thwarted by the TUC General Council's vigilance. While conference believed that policy formation

Photos 28 & 29: (28) A nervous looking Ramsey MacDonald faces the press a week after splitting the Labour Party and forming the National Government with Tories and Liberals. (29) One of the posters for the National Government in the General Election of October 1931 – a bit rich given the cuts in unemployment benefit implemented by them, but, nevertheless, they were swept back to power.

was its own preserve, the National Executive and Parliamentary spokespersons acted in a contrary fashion. The unions' block vote was instrumental in maintaining this regime. And should the block vote prove unreliable occasionally, the National Council of Labour met the day before the National Executive to ensure that any criticism was stifled. By the end of the nineteen-thirties, one of the fastest growing tendencies on the left was the 'Dis-affiliated Constituency Parties' bloc. For, in the absence of political argument, time-honoured methods of expulsion were put into practice. What impact did these national developments have on the Labour Party on Merseyside?

The Labour Party and Liverpool

In Liverpool, the Labour Party in its formative years was a motley collection of interests. A number of socialists joined, especially after the adoption of the 1918 constitution with its now famous Clause Four which made explicit the Labour Party's formal handshake with socialism. Trade union officials and some activists were in the ranks, having joined in sizeable numbers after the big strike wave of 1911 and to a lesser extent, after 1918-20. And there was a large block of support which had transferred allegiance from the Irish Nationalist Party to Labour in the nineteen-twenties. At various times in that decade, the Liverpool Labour Party represented the interests of all three. More frequently, it succeeded in continuing to exist by overlooking the possible contradictions that this diverse constituency created. But the priority was always getting councillors into Castle Street, and MPs into Westminster.

However, the organisational basis for Labour politics was narrow. Electoral support was minimal, centring on four wards – Edge Hill, St. Anne's, Everton, and Garston – in the main, the domicile of regularly employed (as opposed to casually employed) workers. In fact, Liverpool was, up until the thirties, indeed up until 1955, a Tory city.[2] Moreover, at the beginning of the twentieth century, Liverpool was not only deepest blue, but also Orange. For those people of Liverpool who could never ally with either Unionists opposed to Irish independence, or with Tories representing the interests of financiers and shipowners, the alternative was not necessarily "independent labour representation".

Any neat formula that reduces political aspiration and affiliation to class alone, especially in the context of a working class that encompasses many ethnic groups, should be rejected. One quarter of Liverpool's population was Irish or of Irish descent and had considered Irish independence and self-determination to be a decisive political issue. Appeals to class solidarity and class allegiance had no meaning unless "class" meant something other than the concerns of the English working class. This assertion in no way denies the centrality of the Liverpool Irish to collective organisation at the point of production, or on the riverfront. It seeks to explain the very weak resonance that the appeal of "labour representation" had for many Liverpool workers. The British Labour Party had little understanding of the issue of Irish independence and self-determination.

Photo 30: T.P. O'Connor (seated), reading his nomination paper for the 1929 General Election. He was the only Irish Nationalist M.P. in mainland Britain, representing Liverpool Scotland from 1885 until his death six months after the 1929 election. His successor, Davie Logan, was also a Nationalist before converting to Labour in 1923, and represented the area in Parliament until 1964.

As a result, from the later years of the nineteenth century, the Liverpool Irish had supported initially the Liberal Party, and increasingly from 1900 onwards, Irish Nationalist candidates in local and Parliamentary elections. Indeed, until 1929 the North End of the city elected an Irish Nationalist as their Member of Parliament in the Scotland constituency.

The abundant weakness of the Liverpool Labour Party in electoral terms also reflects the ideological weakness of local industrial organisation. The predominantly casual employment of whole sections of the male, and to a certain extent, female working class did not aid the building of stable, formal trade union organisation. As we have seen the thirties were marked by industrial struggle that was directed as much against union leaderships as against employers. Dock work and the shipping industry provide continual examples of the manner in which union officials and employers were locked in mutual support against the interests of the membership. So that, whereas in many other parts of Britain, the Labour Party locally established itself as the 'political voice' of organised labour, on Merseyside tensions within the unions tempered such possibilities. Local Labour politicians did not, and could not rely upon industrial strength to secure electoral success.

Labour and Catholicism

The forced arrival of the twenty-six county Free State in Ireland under the tutelage of Lloyd George in 1921 provided a new backcloth for the Liverpool Labour Party drama. The Nationalist politicians became in rapid succession the Irish Party and then the Centre Party, whose purpose was little more than to become the council mouthpiece of the local Catholic hierarchy. With Ireland now "free", the Catholic aspirations of their electorate became their central concern. Supported by Bishop Keating and the clergy, they translated the widespread support for Irish independence to a narrow conception of interest based upon religion. In a city where Catholics had been systematically discriminated against, this was understandable. But divorced from the struggle against British rule in Ireland, such a movement became embedded in a regressive politics. For example, it was this force of Catholic clergy which organised one of the biggest demonstrations in Liverpool between the wars – 150,000 people in June 1930 protesting against the (Labour) government's bill to raise the school leaving age to fifteen.

In 1928, Bishop Keating died. His most memorable achievement had been the preservation of a separate Catholic political organisation in Liverpool. Soon after his death, a substantial section of the Nationalist rump, who had been recently re-christened again, more appropriately, as the Catholic Representation Association, joined the ranks of the Labour Party. Essentially, the machine of ward politics and divisional parties in the dockside areas had been won by the Labour Party from Nationalist control, but the character and ideology of the machine was unchanged. Councillors who for years had stood as Nationalists, re-appeared draped in Labour colours; but their election addresses and political sympathies remained unchanged.

A year after Keating's death, in addition to winning a majority of the popular vote in the local elections, Labour could claim four Liverpool MPs, and a whole section of councillors almost exclusively now representing the Catholic/Irish wards along the river. But the beginnings of electoral success did not allay ideological division. One Catholic critic speaking of the "fight for the Faith" in 1927 had said of the Labour Party:

"Their meetings are addressed by communists whose slogan is 'no religion in schools'; bands of children are taught ribald songs in Labour centres, Catholic practices are openly jeered at, while the public conscience is being shocked by blasphemous and obscene sentences chalked in legible writing outside Catholic schools and churches."[3]

1929 was a landmark, in as much as it suggested that Labour was no longer marginal in Liverpool, and it represented the organisational amalgamation of two traditions and two political machines – Labourism and the newly re-defined Irish Nationalism. The dockside wards north and south of the Pier Head were now Labour where once they had been green. The councillors by and large remained – the hat they wore every third year on election days, and their party songs, had changed – but little else. The Nationalist politicians were no friends of Irish Republicanism but they clearly voiced an opposition to anti-Catholic sentiment. Labour in Liverpool accepted and adopted itself to Catholic aspirations. But the Catholic hierarchy and many lay people were not prepared to accede to what were perceived to be socialistic tendencies within their new party.

1930 – Cathedrals and Caucuses

The new decade opened with the nascent divisions ready to blossom. Corporation-owned land on the site of the old Brownlow Hill workhouse was to be sold at a knock-down price to the Catholic hierarchy as a site for a cathedral. Labour Party policy demanded that such land should not be sold to private interests, but should be used for housing. The Catholic hierarchy and councillors strongly supported the sale of the land; supporters of official Party policy demurred. The Party on the council split into two opposed factions. The division was about accountability to agreed policy but was complicated by the religious divisions in the Party. Eventually, thirty-two members of the Labour group in the council voted for the sale and only nineteen voted against. The sale went through and resulted in a formal separation of the two factions, both with their own leaders and whips.

A National Executive Committee enquiry three months later awarded the leadership to the supporters of the Cathedral project. This effectively eroded the principle of accountability of the Labour group to the Party. Luke Hogan, right wing trade union official and Catholic, was the uncrowned king of this powerful group.[4]

The consolidation of right wing leadership in the Liverpool Labour Party was, in part, similar to developments throughout the country. The NEC, the TUC leadership in the General Council and the Parliamentary Party attacked dissent with a vehemence that far outweighed their attacks on the National/Tory government. But the form that labour politics took on Merseyside, in particular in Liverpool, was very much the product of local circumstances.

The rules of the game were therefore clear by the thirties. Left wing policy and activity would alienate the Catholic hierarchy, and accordingly would be used to prevent the electoral support of the Catholic working class. So to win that vote, the Labour Party had both to 'moderate' any radical pretensions and to act as an efficient voice of the Catholic hierarchy. The electoral process then determined the policy and activity of the Liverpool Labour Party. If sections of the Party opposed the way the rules were formulated, it was delicately suggested that they keep quiet. If they didn't keep quiet, they were indelicately treated.

To be a radical socialist in Liverpool in the thirties was not easy. For the still sizeable Protestant and Tory working class, if you were Labour, you were a foot soldier of the Vatican dedicated to the Papist domination of Reformation England. Within the Catholic community, you may be portrayed as a pawn of Moscow. For Leo McGree and other members of the Communist Party, the vilification was even more intense. He could expect physical attack from clerical inspired crowds and it was not uncommon for him to have his open air meetings ended by the police "for fears for his own safety".

It is impossible to view the later events in the nineteen-thirties without understanding the nature of divisions in the Labour Party. Class, religion and politics were all thrown together – and the pot was stirred and occasionally warmed by the realities of mass unemployment. In a very real sense, the Labour Party of the period was particularly incapable of resolving the political problems with which it was confronted. At a national level, the election of 1931 with the victory of a National Government led by a former Labour Prime Minister rendered Parliamentary opposition largely irrelevant. Government majorities are rarely defeated, no matter how inspired the oratory. Liverpool Labour had only one representative in the Commons, Davie Logan, MP for the Scotland division of the city.

Locally, the national defeat deprived the Party of any chance of control of the Town Hall for a good number of years. In 1931, the year of defeat and division, Labour won only five out of the forty contested seats at the November council elections, although that did amount to 35% of the popular vote. Additionally, a section of the old Nationalist/Catholic party refused any accord with the Labour Party, and stood for election and won two seats as 'Democratic Labour'.

Town Hall Politics

There was, however, another related but possibly more fundamental reason that suggested Labour was incapable of advance. Political argument and debate was conducted in a vacuum. All protagonists, from Hogan on the right to the Braddocks and Silverman on the left, saw the relationship between the Labour Party and the 'working class' as being straightforward – the Labour Party was the party of the working class. For all the leaders, whether or not the Labour Party articulated and fought for

the interests of the working class and socialist politics was less important than their fight for control of the Party. This, in their view, was the
fight for the 'leadership' of the working class. But the continual feature
of the Liverpool Labour Party throughout the thirties was the absence of
an active, mass membership and popular support. Two National Executive Committee inquiries in 1930 and 1939 into the state of the Party locally both concluded that there was little organic connection between the
Party and the working class. Many of the political issues where division
became public were essentially 'private' issues within the City Council
Labour group.

Liverpool had never had a Labour Lord Mayor. In 1934, such a possibility arose. The Tories, it emerged, were willing to give way and allow
the Labour Party to nominate a person for the exalted office. Secret
meetings were held between White, the Tory boss, Alderman Gates for
the Liberals and Luke Hogan from the Labour Party. A deal was struck.
All parties were to support three men to be made Freemen of the City –
White himself, Bowring, an old rich shipowner, and Alderman James
Sexton, an old trade union boss. In return Labour would be able to nominate their senior alderman for the mayorality.

On 12 September 1934, Fred Richardson was duly proposed. Two
weeks later, the council voted on all the nominations before it. All present voted for the elderly trio to receive their freedoms except for two –
Sidney Silverman and Bessie Braddock. This entirely understandable
objection to honouring political and industrial enemies was supported by
their local ward party, St. Anne's. But the Labour council leadership was
enraged.

Battle ensued. Logan called a meeting of the council group and the
executive of the joint Trades Council and Labour Party. A motion was
put to withdraw the whips from Silverman and Braddock – in effect expelling them from the Labour group. Well over two thirds of the meeting
supported the motion.

This dispute is of minimal importance in its own right. But it illustrated a particular aspect of how the Labour Party operated in Liverpool.
The council group reigned supreme – the 1930 Cathedral dispute had
seen to that. But now the NEC went further and ruled that although the
Trades Council and Labour Party should decide the "general lines of
municipal policy at elections",

"... the council group is entitled to settle its council policy without interference from the Trades Council or any other outside body."[5]

The Trades Council and Labour Party was now nothing more than an outside organisation, which had no formal accountable relationship with elected Labour councillors. They, the council group, were a law unto themselves. Councillors could, if they chose, be responsible to their local wards. But if their ward policy clashed, then the decision of the council group held sway. Silverman and Braddock were re-admitted to the council group after three months but the principle of non-accountability had been further strengthened by the right wing.

One further point is worth making. At the meeting which authorised the expulsions, all Labour councillors and aldermen were present, together with four members of the local Party Executive. All those representing the dockside wards of Sandhills, North and South Scotland, Vauxhall, Great Georges and Brunswick voted for the expulsion of Braddock and Silverman. All these wards were predominantly Catholic. All the councillors were themselves Catholic. None of those who supported the pair were Catholic, and they all represented wards away from the river – Everton, Kirkdale, St. Anne's, Edge Hill and Princes Park. Councillors on both sides were trade union officials, but the defining feature of the meeting – and of the Labour Party – was the religious affiliation of the members concerned. Under Luke Hogan's fierce leadership, religious conviction and outlook fused with a deeply conciliatory civic politics. The language of socialism was rarely heard.

Labour and the Slump

If you occupied a leading position in the Labour Party in Liverpool in the thirties, the certainty was that you were white, very probably male and either a full time trade union officer or a pawnbroker. Davie Logan was a white, male pawnbroker. He was also a dedicated Catholic, having helped to establish the Knights of St Columba in the Scotland Road area. He had also been active in Irish Nationalism before the outbreak of the First World War. He was very much part of the 'shopocracy' of Scotland Road. He would have been hard-pressed to describe himself as a 'socialist', but would have relished that contemporary term, 'a Labour man'. As the sole Labour MP for Liverpool in Parliament in the early thirties, what was he most concerned with? Mass unemployment, the operation of the means test or the economy measures of the recently elected National Government under MacDonald? In December 1931 he told Parliament:

"I come from the city of Liverpool which has a dock line seven miles long, the finest seaport in the world, and when I see the docks idle and find that the shipping is not coming in and when I find that fifty percent of the shipping that does come in is manned with black, Lascar and Arab labour, and that those Britishers who went across the seven seas to fight in the Great War are now, through no fault of their own, walking the streets of Liverpool ... what answer have I to take back? ... Why will no Minister deal with black labour? Why has no Government ever dealt with the question of black, Lascar or Coolie labour that is not British, the employment of which has kept our men walking the streets?"[6]

One year later Logan repeated his chauvinistic comments:

Photo 31: The Crew of the steamer Clan Mackenzie sunk off Liverpool in 1937. They were brought ashore after their vessel collided with another off the Mersey Bar. These were some of the black seafarers that Davie Logan and the National Union of Seamen wanted to keep out of Liverpool.

156

"There are in this House shipowners who boast of the British Empire and who are today carrying aliens, foreigners on their ships. I ask the Government, when are they going to deal with the question of shipping? When are they going to deal with the blacks, the Lascars the aliens who are taking the place of British seamen on British ships? These British seamen are men who went out to the War, who faced the horrors of the deep. They are now standing on the street corners, workless. I am out for the protection of the British race. It is a tragedy to me to walk the streets of our great seaports and to see the men who risked their lives on the sea during the war no longer wanted because cheap labour is preferred, because curry and rice takes the place of roast beef and plum pudding, and because we cannot bring the Britisher down to the curry and rice diet ... Let the Government get back to reality and give these men a right to a livelihood on ships that fly the British flag."[7]

Logan was clearly 'out for the protection of the British race' – an ironic stand for an Irishman. Doubly so if he thought that his British seamen had ever enjoyed a diet of roast beef and plum pudding! He not only demanded that the government 'deal with' black people, but also accused previous governments and shipowners of being not sufficiently patriotic capitalists. Through all his abuse, not one word about the cause of the decline of world trade. Did he draw attention to where Sir John Ellerman, boss of the Ellerman Lines, had accumulated the £17 million which he left in his will in 1933? Did he speak up when unionists on Liverpool boats were being boycotted by the masters and union by the device of the PC5? No, for Logan the enemy was black labour on board ship. Is it any wonder that the black and Chinese communities had little regard for the Liverpool Labour Party? Nationalism and a vengeful patriotism supplanted any concept of internationalism, and the racism of the Empire was forcefully reflected by Liverpool's sole Labour representative in Parliament.

Garden Festivals in the Eighties, Fishing Ports in the Thirties

But what kind of policies were the party putting forward locally? They remained woven in a web of parochialism. The most absurd manifestation of this was the following pledge in the 1932 manifesto:

"If elected, the city council should mount an immediate investigation into the viability of Liverpool as a fishing port."[8]

Two years later the Tories took up this bright idea:

"... the shadowy outline of a great fishing industry for the port is discernible through the mists of the future ... the prime objectives are to provide employment, utilise the unrivalled facilities of the Mersey and to enable the city to supply itself with a valuable article of food at a minimum cost."[9]

A few years later notices were erected on the Hoylake shore drawing attention to the danger of eating fish caught locally! Just one example of how harebrained schemes acquired substance in the absence of clear socialist strategy.

This was the era of municipalisation, when solutions to impoverishment were seen to lie in taking the milk supply into council ownership, creating a municipal orchestra and building open-air swimming pools and sports stadia. All admirable aims, of course, but in the absence of a politically coherent campaign against the policies of central government they never attained serious conviction. The Labour Party's acceptance of a strategy based solely on gaining power in Parliament determined the policies it presented to the electorate. "Wait until the next general election and the return of a Labour government" was the cry. "And then ..." In the meantime the people were not convinced that a fishing industry would solve the overwhelming problems of poverty and unemployment on Merseyside.

The failure of the Labour Party to fight effectively for the unemployed was sadly demonstrated in 1935. As we saw in Chapter Five, the National Government aimed to undercut the increasingly successful work in local areas to force Public Assistance Committees to pay benefits above the nationally recommended levels. The Unemployment Bill of 1934, which established the Unemployed Assistance Board, was clearly intended to remove the setting of benefit levels from local political control. Initially the Liverpool Labour Party opposed this change. Deputations were sent to London, speeches were made in the Council chamber, petitions were organised, but all to no avail. When the Bill was eventually put into effect in early 1935, it rapidly became clear that the UAB signified dramatic cuts in benefit. The Labour Party's own newspaper, the *Daily Herald*, had already disarmed its readers by assuring them that such cuts would not happen when the bill was implemented. When the NUWM called for mass demonstrations against the changes, the Labour Party nationally remained unmoved. Locally the Labour Party, despite their previous fine speeches against the bill, refused to be associated with a campaign of direct action against the benefit cuts.

We have already seen that the public outcry organised by the NUWM amongst the unemployed forced the Government to back down. The Standstill Act was passed which temporarily at least restored benefit levels.

"The Standstill Act of 1935 was the greatest victory achieved by the agitation of the unemployed since the immediate post-war years."[10]

This claim, by a recent writer on these events, is a necessary emphasis in that it clearly shows that the unemployed were independently active and not just "acted upon". But in Liverpool as elsewhere, the Labour Party could claim no great role in this victory for the unemployed. In fact during the period of late 1934 and early 1935 the local Labour Party was far more concerned with expelling left wing councillors over the "freedom of the city" issue. At the height of the campaign over the UAB, in a Parliamentary by-election in Wavertree, it was reported that:

"The Labour campaign has been conducted throughout on what has been described as a Sunday school pattern – quiet and studiously impeccable. There has been scarcely a mention of socialism; no outdoor meetings and no Sunday meetings."[11]

Ironically Labour won the by-election, mainly because the Tory vote was split by an Independent candidate, and also perhaps because Labour stood a staunch Methodist in a predominantly non-Catholic seat. A triumph for the Parliamentary concerns of the Party, perhaps, but at the time of no great significance to the unemployed of the city.

The Labour Left
There was another side to the Liverpool Labour Party, however. It was comprised of individuals in the Party who were happy to be known as socialists. But when they argued for socialist politics in the thirties, they did not only have to decry and vilify the actions of central government and their supporters locally. There were enemies even closer to home.

Take the case of Sidney Silverman who won the nomination for Labour candidate in the Exchange constituency by-election of 1933. The left within the party were able to secure Silverman's selection from their base of support in St.Anne's ward. The constituency was overwhelmingly working class in composition, despite a sizeable minority of Tory business voters, and it was predominantly Catholic.

In the campaign Silverman led a vigorous attack on the policies of the National Government: over the imprisonment of Tom Mann the veteran socialist whose connections with the local labour movement went back to 1911 when he had chaired the Central Strike Committee of the Transport Strike; over the implementation of the so called economy measures and the means test; over the imposition of trade protectionism as a way out of economic depression. Whilst he did not pretend that free trade was an adequate answer to all our difficulties, he said:

"... If under Free Trade you are lashed with a whip, under Protection you are lashed with a scorpion,"[12]

An apt comment for those advocating import controls today. Silverman, then, fought the campaign as a socialist. Catholic councillors in the area became apprehensive. A leaflet was distributed outside all Catholic churches on the Sunday before polling:

"We are finally and personally convinced that you, our working class people – man and women in Exchange, will be well advised to vote for Colonel Shute (the Tory candidate) for the following reasons:

1. because as Catholics you cannot accept the extreme socialist policy of Mr. Silverman. It is not sound – it is not good for our working classes.

2. you cannot expect Mr. Silverman to further the just claims of our Catholic schools."[13]

All ten local councillors signed it, all ten Catholics and all ten anti-socialists (including Peter Kavanagh, whose name lives on today in a pub in Egerton Street). Shute, a Catholic Tory, won the election, although his majority was cut from 13,100 to 2,700. Silverman wrote a postscript:

"It is a triumph of religious prejudice over political ambitions. My opponent throughout fought his campaign purely on a religious basis and managed to persuade enough hungry, ill-clad, and badly-housed people, suffering unparalleled privations at the hands of the National Government, to ignore the fact that Colonel Shute is pledged to support that Government, and vote for him purely on the basis of the similarity of their religious beliefs."[14]

On this occasion then a determined attempt by the left in the local Labour Party to lead a campaign against government policies was crushed by the wheeling in of the religious question and the working class continued to suffer.

The campaign to enforce party policy on frequently unwilling advocates, was a continual feature of labour politics in the thirties. From
1932, a small section of the Labour left had been working politically
with the local National Unemployed Workers Movement branches on
both sides of the Mersey. It was not rare for the NUWM to clash with
Labour nominees on the Public Assistance Committees. In 1936, Bessie
Braddock was censured by the Labour leadership for making accusations against a Labour member of the PAC.[15] Two years later, she was
again up before an internal party inquiry for alleged remarks and actions
whilst speaking at an NUWM street meeting in the North End, itself an
offence. In particular, she was said to have made public, derogatory remarks about two local Labour councillors – Sheehan and Reppion. Reppion alleged that Braddock made the following statement from the platform:

> "I do not know what your people are doing up here at this end on the housing question,
> but from what I can see not very much. We can always be seen in St. Anne's every Tues-
> day...and if you cannot find them up here to do the job, get rid of them and get somebody
> who can. I suppose when I have finished up clearing up the bottom end they will want me
> to come up here and straighten this end out. You want organisation. I do not care which
> party you join – whether it's the Communist Party, the United Front or the Labour Party –
> but get in something!"[16]

Bessie denied the charge, but the allegations were upheld. The rules
of the Party – standing order number 2 – ruled against any councillor
making "public or semi-public attacks on any other member of the group
which damages the standing of the Party". Do it again, she was warned,
and you'll be out.

Most revealing of all the exchanges in the inquiry was the following
minute:

> "Councillor Reppion (South Scotland ward) was then questioned and he intimated that he
> took exception to Mrs Braddock addressing meetings in the ward, without invitation
> from the Division or ward association. There is no ward association at present in South
> Scotland, nor has there been for the last twelve months."

Reppion and Sheehan were secure in the knowledge that with no
ward organisation, they would not be de-selected. And Bessie Braddock
knew that the only way such councillors would be removed was if
people joined the Party. On the whole, the working class was content to

watch and occasionally support the Labour Party, and rarely to make any greater committment. Ironically, only fifteen years in the nineteen-fifties, Bessie Braddock was assisting the McCartheyite witch-hunting against the left.

Ultimately the Labour Party in Liverpool in the nineteen-thirties existed in a vacuum very much of its own making. In the absence of mass involvement it could not explain and resolve the issues that mass unemployment imposed on the working class. Socialist rhetoric collapsed into a style of politics that singularly failed to mount a serious challenge to the prevailing economic orthodoxies. The unemployed bore the brunt of that failure.

Notes
1. J. Saville, 'May Day 1937', *Essays in Labour History, 1918-1939*, Eds. A. Briggs & J. Saville (London, Croom Helm, 1977).
2. R.S.W. Davies, 'The Liverpool Labour Party and the Liverpool Working Class, 1900-1939', *NWLHS Bulletin*, No.6, 1979-80, p.2.
3. *Liverpool Daily Post*, 22.10.1927.
4. MSRG, *Merseyside in Crisis* (Liverpool, 1980), p.79.
5. *Liverpool Daily Post*, 9.1.1935.
6. Hansard, 9.12.1931.
7. Hansard, 8.11.1932.
8. *Liverpool Daily Post*, 14.10.1932.
9. Liverpool Conservative Party, *Progressive Liverpool* (1934), p.8.
10. J. Hinton, *Labour and Socialism: A History of the British Labour Movement 1867-1974* (Brighton, Wheatsheaf, 1983), p.151.
11. *Liverpool Daily Post*, 2.2.1935.
12. *Liverpool Daily Post*, 5.1.1933.
13. *Liverpool Daily Post*, 16.1.1933.
14. *Liverpool Daily Post*, 20.1.1933.
15. *Liverpool City Council Group Meeting Minutes*, 2.6.1936.
16. *Liverpool City Council Group Meeting Minutes*, 11.3.1938

11
STYLES OF REACTION: ORANGEISM AND FASCISM IN THE THIRTIES

In January 1928 a Reverend Armitage turned to a time-honoured theme in his address to the congregation of Christ Church, Church of England, in Great Homer Street:

> "In one day picked at random there were 47,054 individuals signing on at labour exchanges ... in addition 60,266 received out-relief from the guardians ... The fact is that Liverpool is over-populated ... There is the menace of the Irish...The Irish have shouted for Home Rule but tens of thousands of them refuse to stay at home. In one recent year 44,150 people of the working class type left Ireland for Liverpool. 37,000 of the same type returned from Liverpool to Ireland, leaving 6,450 individuals who have remained."[1]

Four months later, the Tory Lord Mayor of the year, Margaret Beavan, took herself off on an official visit to Italy. She met Mussolini, was pictured with him giving the fascist salute and then described him as "one of the greatest I have ever met".[2] At the June City Council meeting a huge row broke out when she revealed she had taken it upon herself to invite him to Liverpool. But the Labour Party, to its eternal credit, made certain that the Mersey never had to carry *Il Duce*. These two seemingly unconnected events were illustrative of the dual nature of the politics of reaction on Merseyside in the nineteen-thirties.

Working class consciousness has never been a clean, unsullied piece of paper on which socialism attempts to make an imprint. Certainly, British history has left a very real mark on that consciousness. A 'commonsense' which comprehends the world, but does not always explain that world in the same way as the socialist movement. The left in the thirties had to popularise its own analysis and strategy and, additionally, argue with political forces that sought to explain the depression in other ways. In Liverpool these political forces, whether Tory, Orange or openly fascist, attempted to prevent the growth of class unity by inflating the existing divisions within the working class. Economic depression, slump and unemployment do not lead automatically to a leftward radicalisation of political sentiment. The British nation and the empire, race and the family can be invoked as institutions to be defended. The story goes that these have made Britain what it is. In Liverpool there was no shortage of tendencies and political organisations of a reactionary nature who were willing to ascribe the causes of mass unemployment to a failure to preserve these institutions, and the encouraging of divisions within the working class. Fascism reiterated the dual themes of nationalism and anti-semitism, whilst Orangeism fuelled anti-Irish and anti-Catholic bigotry. The establishment, too, strengthened racist and sexist sentiment in the period. Why should women work when men are unemployed? Why, when "Englishmen" have to apply to the Parish, should black people still be in jobs? Why, indeed, should they be in the country at all? Tragically, such poisonous ideas were echoed in sections of the working class. All this in a decade when fascism and nationalism were increasingly taking hold throughout Europe. But these developments did not go unopposed. The battle against Franco in Spain, on the one hand, and against the British Union of Fascists in the East End of London, on the other, mark the profile of anti-fascist struggle. No Passaran! "They shall not pass" echoed from Madrid to Cable Street.

English Protestantism and the Irish in Liverpool

The Reverend Armitage was not the first Protestant churchman to try to make political capital out of a spurious statistical correlation between criminality, people on relief, unemployment and the "the continued Irish influx". But as the slump deepened so the chorus of voices which suggested that the Irish were the root of the problem increased. These voices were not confined to the Orange fringe. The Church of England hierarchy in the Liverpool diocese played a prominent part in the campaign.

Canon Charles E. Raven opened with a seemingly innocuous piece in the Diocesan publication, the *Liverpool Review*, under the title of "The Irish Problem". He remarked that the year of 1930 marked the end of Liverpool's prosperity and contended that "the religious and racial bitterness for which our city has been unpleasantly notorious is undoubtedly increasing in violence". He asserted that "there is a widespread belief that our social progress is being hampered and our financial stringency increased by the influx of immigrants from the Irish Free State.[3] The apparent innocence of his request for a "public discussion of these issues" in fact represented a sophisticated campaign to bolster anti-Irish sentiment. Within three short months he claimed to have the "information" he was after. This suggested that immigration and settlement of the Irish in Liverpool was growing rapidly; "that every form of public or private assistance is very seriously burdened by (our Irish invaders') claims upon it; that the Irish people who come to Liverpool were of the 'lowest class'; and that the Irish were responsible for a large percentage of crime".[4] In fact such "information" relating to nationality was not kept by the authorities and his conclusions were based entirely on prejudice and hearsay. Under the cloak of reasoned argument and rational debate, the reason for Liverpool's demise had been located – the Irish. Restriction on Irish immigration was his solution. Three years later the Liverpool Review moved the pace of this invidious campaign forward. One G.M. Blair wrote a venomous piece entitled, "The Irish immigration question". He concluded:

"There is a real alien menace, as is clear from the study of any of our populations in the great cities...but the greatest feature of this alien menace lies in immigration into Britain during the last hundred years of Irish Mediterranean stock. This is a definite menace, not because these people are undesirable in their own habitat, but because they are in that of the Nordic race (sic). There, their presence can only bring a repetition of some of those worst features which we have experienced in Ireland."

Remember this was not the street corner Orange rag but the official mouthpiece of the Church of England in Liverpool. The conclusion was spelt out:

"The United States, seeing her institutions likely to crumble before this menace, and with the glaring lesson of the deleterious effects of 'wops', 'dagoes' and Irish in her lower orders, has with admirable courage closed the doors and adopted a policy which aims at the maintenance of the Nordic race-type...and Britain would do well to make a careful note of it, and not only that, but act accordingly."[5]

This Anglican view of the superiority of the "Nordic race" was not far removed from the notion of the "master race" and "Aryan purity" of German nazism. The quasi-scientific arguments of the Liverpool Review underlay the call for the prohibition of Irish immigration. The Anglican clergy were unable to conceal their blatant prejudice.

This campaign found substantial support. The Tory M.P.s for Liverpool continually pressed their government with demands for an end to immigration and the deportation of Irish people who became unemployed in Liverpool. By 1939, an "official" report of the Economic League, a body of industrialists, was commissioned to inquire into the causes and extent of unemployment in Liverpool. The findings were given much prominence, both in the local press and in Parliament:

"... they (the Irish) appear to prefer remaining here on the dole, with occasional jobs, to returning to their own country. Once here, they tend to stay and in many cases are said to bring their relatives over from Ireland to share their good fortune at the expense of the British taxpayers and ratepayers."[6]

Only two months later the Liverpool Chamber of Commerce, representing local businessmen, echoed these sentiments in their monthly magazine:

"... Irish imported labour falls back on the English dole, having first deprived English labour of employment and after having been over in England long enough to qualify for the dole. This imported Irish labour deprives our people of work and takes unemployment pay out of the British taxpayer and working man."[7]

Three months later a group of Tory councillors weighed in with a report by their *Irish Immigration Investigation Bureau* (*sic*), repeating the same kind of allegations.[8] Ireland had been systematically ravaged for over one hundred years to provide British industry with a steady supply of labour. When that labour was no longer required, Ireland was held responsible for the creation of mass unemployment.

In this atmosphere, the Protestant fringe of Orange churches, bible classes and lodges, were not slow to take up the war cry. Protestant councillors were elected throughout the thirties with Tory support in Netherfield and St. Domingo wards in Everton. Slogans which had been mobilising agents before the 1914 war – the Reformation, the sanctity of the prayer book and the oath of accession – were jettisoned and replaced by "No Irish in Liverpool". In 1937, the Protestant Party contested the local election on the basis of the "no grants for Catholic schools" – or at least that was the ostensible campaign. One of their leaflets in St. Domingo gives the full vehemence of the message:

"The Labour Party wants to subsidise a foreign religion – Popery – and give £545,000 for papist schools. The Labour Party builds houses and tenements for Irish aliens but objected to St. Domingo Tenements being kept for St. Domingo folk. The Labour Party encourages immigration. The Labour Party wanted an Irish Papist Lord Mayor – Hogan – so that he could boost Dr. Downey's cathedral and fly the Pope's flag over the Town Hall."[9]

'By Their Friends, So Shall You Know Them'

Throughout the twenties and thirties the leading public figure associated with the Orange movement in Liverpool was Pastor H.D. Longbottom. His Protestant Reform Church on Netherfield Road and his speaker's platform at St. Domingo's Pit were the centres of militant Protestantism. As an Alderman he had a platform for his bigotry in the council chambers throughout the thirties. In 1923 Longbottom's church magazine, *The Protestant Reformer*, carried a report of a meeting at which Longbottom had shown clear support for the Ku Klux Klan.

> "... they appear to desire that America should be 100% American and strongly Protestant. So far as its main principles go, I find myself in agreement with them."[10]

One month later it was added that:

> "We are in touch with American leaders regarding the KKK and have interesting facts to disclose. A branch is to be formed in England and we can honestly say that we see nothing in its constitution contrary to Christian teaching, true patriotism and the highest form of citizenship."[11]

Only four years previously the race riots in Liverpool had culminated in the death of a black seaman, Charles Wooton – echoes of the KKK lynchings of the southern United States.

Exhortations to purge Liverpool of "papist scum" and "aliens" were common amongst the fringe bigots of the Protestant community. Attempts to deny the right to work on the basis of nationality and colour were not new. The local Conservative Party had historically used such arguments to retain electoral support in the Protestant areas. The unemployment of the nineteen thirties served to heighten the clamour of such calls. The Anglican Church, the Tory Party and increasingly the Government joined in the witchhunt. While the Anti-Fascist Committee may have been successful in preventing the emergence of a co-ordinated fascist movement on Merseyside by street actions, who challenged the state in its removal of Chinese or African seamen from Britain and the deportation of Irish men and women forced onto relief? Orangeism, then, was one powerful tendency on Mersey which sought to extend the divisions within the working class in order to defeat class unity. The relationship of the Orange fringe with the other major tendency – the fascist movement – was a complex one. While *The Protestant Reformer* viewed the

167

KKK favourably, Orangeism could not embrace wholeheartedly the fascist movement of the nineteen-thirties. In 1937, *The Protestant Times* condemned the "Communist murderous attack on Sir Oswald Mosley, fascist chief", but added:

> "We hate Fascism, believing it to be born of priestly dictatorialism and tyranny, but we desire with all our soul to protest against the murderous gang of hooligans brought up from Scotland and St. Anne's wards to smash up the Fascist chief."[12]

The Orange papers and organisations clearly viewed fascism as another extension of world domination by the Vatican, given the close identification of the Catholic Church with the fascist rebellion in the Spanish Civil War. Nevertheless, the British Union of Fascists (B.U.F.) and the Orange Lodges undeniably had certain ideas in common. The search for a scapegoat was one thing which united them, although they differed as to who should be that scapegoat.

The Blackshirts on Merseyside

A number of prominent individuals in Liverpool, like Margaret Beavan, were attracted to fascist ideas. During the general election campaign in 1929, there were continual accusations from the Labour Party that Tory candidates, especially Sir James Reynolds in Exchange constituency, were using "fascists" to viciously steward public meetings.[13] But it was really in 1933, when the B.U.F. and Mosley, supported by William Joyce (later Lord Haw-Haw of Nazi fame in the War) began to take their politics around the country, that Liverpool was directly confronted by the ideology of fascism. In November 1933, Joyce addressed the first B.U.F. rally in the Stadium. 6,000 people heard him espouse the soon familiar theme of the stranglehold that "international financiers" – in other words Jews and the "unpatriotic" British shipowners who were employing "coloured labour" on British ships – had on the British economy. The beginnings of the pro-German position of the B.U.F. were clear when he called for the suppression of Jewish-owned picture houses. The issues were established on which the B.U.F. were to campaign – the "alien threat"; slump and unemployment arising from a Jewish conspiracy and unpatriotic capitalists; and agitation against those aspects of British society that supposedly attacked British "liberty" – trade unionism and socialism, the "Red Menace".[14]

The following year the fascists organised a meeting in the Stadium again. The anti-fascist movement was not prepared to let it take place unopposed and planned a march from Islington Square, down through town, past the Stadium to a rally on the Dock Road. The Anti Fascist Committee (AFC) was a successful popular front of Communist and Independent Labour Party members, National Unemployed Workers Movement branches and some members of the Labour Party. The Liverpool police saw the AFC march, rather than the BUF meeting, as a possible source of trouble. With their usual partiality, they allowed the Blackshirts to hold their rally and banned the anti-fascist demonstration. The AFC were determined to fight the ban but telegrams to and audiences with the Lord Mayor brought no joy. The AFC went ahead with plans for a march. By six o'clock on Sunday, 21st October, a crowd had assembled which 'covered the greater part of Islington square'. The only named speaker at the rally, Charles Heaton, set the tune for the illegal demonstration that was to be attempted:

"Stand in ranks. If any incident does occur do not involve yourselves in it. This is a demonstration against fascism. It is not a mischief-making or trouble-making demonstration."[15]

Several hundred people formed up to leave the square after the Bootle contingent had arrived. The way out to Shaw Street was blocked by a strong cordon of police and when the anti-fascists tried to move out the other way into Salisbury Street, the police moved in, grabbed the banners, made a number of arrests and dispersed the crowd. Despite attempts to re-form on London Road and in town the police were sufficiently well-organised, with large reserves, to prevent the protest against the Blackshirts taking place. Outside the Stadium things were different. All streets were guarded by police and no-one was allowed to pass into the vicinity of the Stadium without a ticket. Inside the hall fascist discipline reigned. The *Daily Post* reporter saw many interruptions in the first half hour but these "were not allowed to proceed". Those who interrupted were immediately surrounded by blackshirted stewards and were either escorted or forcibly ejected from the hall. There was a large force of police on duty outside and a prison van waited in a side street.[16] Fascist violence inside the meetings was buttressed by police vigilance outside. The fascists left the Stadium and were escorted back to their "headquarters" in Duke Street by the police. Some of the blackshirts spent that evening differently. One, William Twist, an unemployed salesman from

Walton, was addressing a crowd in Tithebarn Street with cries of "Up the Blackshirts, down with the Redshirts and to hell with the Jews." He was charged with being drunk and disorderly and fined 10s. Less than twelve months later, the fascists were to claim their first victim. Whilst most of their visible public activity was centred on big meetings at the Stadium, smaller local meetings were also held, where their armoured vans doubled as speakers' platforms. At one such meeting in Bootle in June 1935, a hostile crowd of 500 gathered at Church View when a fascist van appeared. At the end of the meeting the twelve blackshirts who had protected the van began to climb aboard to depart when stones were thrown, and fighting broke out. The Chief Constable's version of the story from thereon reads:

> "The police separated the combatants and the van moved off through the crowd, its progress being facilitated by the police. It then came to the knowledge of the police that a woman had fainted."[17]

In fact the woman was Frances Evans and she had not fainted but was dead! Meanwhile, the van was chased down Irlam Road to the fascist headquarters on the Strand Road where every window was broken. Whether this was connected with the death of Frances Evans is not known. But at the Coroner's inquest another twist unfolded. An anonymous letter was received in which the author said he was present at the meeting and the trouble had started in the crowd when a blackshirted steward was seen to strike a 'half-caste' child without any reason.[18]

The British Union of Fascists tried to organise large rallies in Liverpool on two further occasions. Both times the anti-fascist forces were able to rally mass support for their demonstrations. In October 1936, the BUF had applied for and won police approval for a military-style march from the Adelphi Hotel, through town, to the Stadium. 300 blackshirts assembled on Lewis's corner in full uniform – peaked caps, black tunics, riding breeches, with streak of lightning badges on scarlet armlets.

One of their armoured vans had knocked over an elderly man on Lime Street before the march had set off and the vast crowd of anti-fascist demonstrators saw this as a further provocation. Fighting broke out and the waiting mounted police were called in to "restore order". The anti-fascist opposition, however, was large enough to prevent Mosley taking the salute of the blackshirts on Lime Street. All along the route of

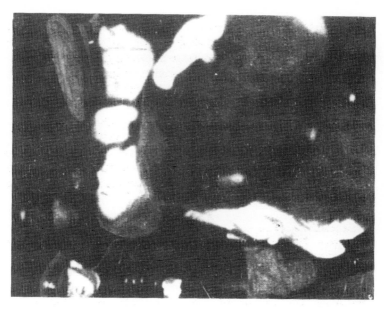

Photos 32 & 33: Scenes at the fascist meeting in the Liverpool Stadium in October 1936. (32) The fascists marching down Lime Street, heavily protected by police. Note the military style uniforms and Union Jacks. (33) A wounded fascist is carried away from the fracas at the Stadium. Again note the uniform.

the march the fascists were subject to a constant hail of bricks and numerous attempts were made to break into the column. On Lime Street, St. John's Lane, Whitechapel, Exchange Street East and at the Stadium, the anti-fascists tried to stop the parade. At every point the strong force of police, co-ordinated for the first time by a loud speaker car, defended the fascists.

The scene at the stadium starkly resembled scenes at Nuremburg. Spotlights lit the platform while the hall was shrouded in darkness. A massive white sheet was stretched from half-way down the hall up onto the platform, surrounded by Union Jacks and massive portraits of Mosley. All the fascist symbols – strength, leadership and order – were represented in the scene. Mosley was able to reiterate the vicious themes of fascism: the threat of "red violence"; unemployment; the erosion of trade with the Empire "driving wages down to coolie levels", and the "alien" Jewish menace to Britain:

> "Those Jews who put the interest of the Jewry before those of Britain will have to get out. The Jews have organised a nation within a nation. Those who remain will be treated as they have elected by their conduct to be treated..."[19]

A clear incitement to follow the Nazi path. The state exacted retribution from the anti-fascists for their organised opposition. Twelve were tried at the Police Courts in Dale Street. Two men were jailed for two months and the others were given stiff fines. Thomas Kennedy, a sixty-one year old labourer from Dingle Lane was singled out for special treatment. He was charged with being armed with an offensive weapon, an ornamental sword, on Lime Street and, according to the police, being disorderly, shouting, "We want Mosley. We don't want them in Liverpool. Let's stop the bastards". In court his philosophy became clearer:

> "I am very, very sorry sir and that's all I have to say. I will say nothing against the police. It's been plaguing my mind, this here man trying to make my town and city another Hitler and Spain. We're going through enough. He should be doing time. He wants to take the Kings place, that's what he does."

His previous convictions were ascertained – thirty-two offences, mostly for drunkeness and assault. He was given two months hard labour and said, as he went below:

"Thank you sir and I hope to be good for you. Back Woodstock for the Cesarewitch. Good day and God bless you."[20]

On the one hand, Thomas Kennedy could be dismissed as a drunk, a joker. But, on the other hand, it is clear that the popular opposition to Mosley and fascism in Liverpool had a very wide base. The anti-fascist movement attracted support from many sections of the working class, and this was illustrated most dramatically in the following year.

The battle of Cable Street, and the million people who stopped the blackshirts marching through the East End of London, took place in 1936, the same year as Franco's Nationalist coup in Spain. It seemed that the issue of fascism was more and more predominant. But the BUF in Britain were fighting a losing battle. The attempt to appease the "nationalist" movement while becoming increasingly consolidated into the "fascist international" was proving to be a major handicap in the battle for popular support. Besides which, the British ruling class were not at all disillusioned with the rule of the National/Tory governments. In 1936 Mosley had organised a march in Liverpool the week after Cable Street, and in 1937 he came to Liverpool a week after mass opposition to fascism erupted in Bermondsey. He was due to speak in Walton on some vacant land by Queens Drive.

An hour before Mosley was due to speak, the Communist party had already organised a public meeting on the same piece of ground. The crowd swelled until 10,000 people were present by the time the fascist speaking van/armoured car drew up. As soon as an electrician appeared to erect the loudspeaker, stones and bricks began to be thrown at the van. Mosley then climbed onto the platform. He had been there for only two minutes and had yet to speak when a brick struck him on the temple, knocking him unconscious. At this stage mounted police appeared from Corporation yard to clear the crowd with maximum violence. Mosley was taken to Walton Hospital. The rumour was that he was unconscious for only thirty minutes and needed only three stitches. Nevertheless, he was kept in for five days, presumably to secure maximum publicity as a victim of "red violence", but perhaps also to escape further attack when he came out.

A number of arrests of anti-fascists were made that day, including one man chained to his bike![21] Several were fined, all of whom referred to

Photos 34, 35 & 36: Scenes at the BUF meeting on Queens Drive, Walton, in 1937. (34) Above: Sir Oswald Mosley addressing the crowd from the top of a van. (35) Opposite: Mosley being carried off the van after being struck on the head by a stone. (36) Opposite: A bandaged Mosley leaving Walton Hospital several days later.

Photo 35

Photo 36

the brutality of the police in clearing the meeting, One man, George Melander, was charged with "wounding Sir Oswald Mosley with intent to do grievous bodily harm". In the trial it rapidly became obvious that Melander was being framed by the police to cover their failure to protect Mosley satisfactorily. He was acquitted on all charges. Mosley's wounding marked the end of fascist activity on Merseyside. Clearly, this was linked to the demise of the BUF in Britain, but it was also an index of the strength of the organised opposition to Mosley locally.

Notes
1. *Liverpool Daily Post*, 9.1.1928.
2. *Liverpool Daily Post*, 31.5.1928.
3. *Liverpool Review*, May 1931 pp.166-7.
4. *Liverpool Review*, August 1931 pp.268-71.
5. *Liverpool Review*, January 1934.
6. *Liverpool Daily Post*, 2.3.1939.
7. *The Liverpool Trade Review*, May 1939, p.117.
8. Irish Immigration Investigation Bureau, *Report*, 1939.
9. Protestant Leaflet, 1937, Liverpool Local History Library, 331/TRA 17.
10. *Protestant Reformers' Monthly Magazine*, February, 1923.
11. *Protestant Reformers' Monthly Magazine*, March, 1923.
12. *Protestant Times*, 16.10.1937.
13. *Liverpool Daily Post*, 22.5.1929; 29.5.1929.
14. *Liverpool Daily Post*, 27.11.1933
15. *Liverpool Daily Post*, 22.10.1934; *Daily Worker*, 22.10.1934.
16. *Liverpool Daily Post*; *Daily Worker*, 22.10.1934.
17. *Liverpool Daily Post*, 26.6.1935.
18. *Liverpool Daily Post*, 26.6.1935.
19. *Liverpool Daily Post*, 12.10.1936.
20. *Liverpool Daily Post*, 13.10.1936.
21. *Liverpool Daily Post*, 11.10.1937.

12
THE UNEMPLOYED FIGHT BACK: THE NUWM IN LIVERPOOL

While the traditional image of the thirties is one of depression and defeat for the working class, there is one positive sign of working class resistance that will always be associated with the "low, dishonest decade": the hunger march. The name of Jarrow still remains the most powerful reminder of the social disaster of the thirties's depression, because the hunger march of the Jarrow crusaders in 1936 made such a deep impression on public opinion. But even though it remains such a powerful symbol, the Jarrow march was a relatively small affair compared with the national hunger marches of the thirties, which saw thousands of the unemployed from all over the country walking to London to press the demands of the unemployed on an unsympathetic Parliament. Behind these marches, organising them, building support for them, publicising them, was the National Unemployed Workers Movement (NUWM). For that achievement alone the NUWM would be worth remembering, but in fact the hunger marches were only the most dramatic examples of NUWM activity. At a local level, throughout the country, the NUWM was also involved in the day to day organising of the unemployed which ensured that they had a voice through the thirties. It is for this reason that the NUWM can be seen as one of the few real "successes" for the working class in a decade of defeats.

But not everybody saw it like that at the time. In 1935 Alderman Simon Mahon, at that time a Labour councillor in Bootle and later the Labour M.P. for Bootle, had this to say about the NUWM:

> "They are irresponsible leaders who are urging these young people to get every penny they can out of the Corporation. We are £22,000 overspent and these people are going around hindering us when we are doing the best for them. They are taking a mean, despicable advantage in saying that one of our officials has "cooked" the balance sheet to "kid" the auditor. The officials are tied down and cannot speak for themselves ... We have not been driven, nor do we intend to be driven, by any irresponsible body ... Notes have been sent to the chairman, deputy chairman and the members of the Public Assistance Committee in filthy and slanderous language ... I think that this Council should put the matter into the hands of somebody who can deal with it."[1]

Photo 37: The crowd at Islington Square during the unemployed riots in Liverpool in September 1932.

The Bootle branch of the NUWM, the "irresponsible body" that Alderman Mahon was complaining about, was at the time pressing the PAC to raise the level of relief payments which stood at the princely sum of 17s for single men, 15s for single women, and 26s for a married couple, rising to 30s if they had two children. Looking back from our vantage point today, Mahon's hostility to the NUWM seems barely credible. Here was a representative of the working class complaining of the "irresponsibility" of an organisation fighting to improve benefits for the vast numbers of the unemployed in the area. What is even more puzzling is that Mahon was by no means untypical of the leading ranks of the Labour movement locally and nationally. Fundamentally, the Labour Party and the Trade Union Movement was at best unsympathetic and at worst downright hostile to the main organisation of the unemployed. In that context the successes the NUWM are all the more remarkable. But it also raises another question. How much more successful might the NUWM have been in advancing the claims of the unemployed if it had had the wholehearted support of the organised labour movement? To explain the tragic failure of the TUC and Labour Party to support the organised unemployed in the thirties we need to trace the history of the NUWM itself.

Organising the Unemployed

"The task of organising the unemployed is not a simple one. One has first to contend with the fact that it is difficult for a person to think of his unemployment as a permanent feature of his life. It is a condition from which he is always striving to get away. In the field of unemployment it is only at critical moments when his standard is being attacked that he feels the need for the strength of organisation which he can only gain by combination with his fellows who are in a like position."[2]

There is a long history of efforts to organise the unemployed on Merseyside. The Clarion Van of the ILP in the eighteen-nineties doling out soup to the unemployed on St. George's Plateau was a regular reminder to the worthy citizens of one of the richest cities in the British Empire that unemployment was endemic and brought with it poverty, malnutrition and ill-health. In the years immediately after the First World War a local Unemployed Committee organised the unemployed. By 1921 it was holding demonstrations almost daily, culminating in an occupation of the Walker Art Gallery to publicise the plight of the unemployed, during which Jack Braddock, among others, was arrested.

However, it was the establishment of the NUWM which provided the first permanent organisation specifically to defend the rights and standards of living of the unemployed. Activities similar to those in Liverpool were mirrored in many areas of the country in the period 1920-21, most notably in Poplar in London, where George Lansbury's leadership of a campaign against the unfair burden that poor boroughs had to bear in paying Poor Relief, gave rise to the term "Poplarism". It was out of this spreading national agitation that the NUWM sprang in April 1921. Its first conference in London had representatives from over sixty local Unemployed Committees, and in its early years it coordinated activity throughout the country. It published a paper, 'Out of Work', and in late 1922 it organised the first National Hunger March to

London, on which Liverpool provided a contingent of unemployed workers. Moreover, in these early years the NUWM had some success in forging links with the Trade Union movement. The 1923 TUC conference set up a Joint Advisory Committee with the NUWM, despite the fact that many of the leading figures of the NUWM were members of the Communist Party (C.P.).

After this promising start, the NUWM made little progress in the mid-twenties. Its membership fell, and its paper collapsed in 1924. It also lost support from the trade union movement. A motion at the 1924 TUC Conference to affiliate the NUWM was heavily defeated, and after July 1925 the TUC refused to send delegates to the JAC, eventually dissolving it in 1927. This decision reflected the rightward shift by the TUC after 1926. The movement was forced back onto the defensive, and moderation was the order of the day. This trend drew the TUC into conflict with the National Minority Movement, a rank and file organisation within the unions which was strongly supported by the CP, and relations between the TUC and the CP deteriorated. In this context it was predictable that the TUC wanted nothing to do with the NUWM, given its strong connections with the CP. Thus from 1927 the distant relationship between the NUWM and the "official" labour movement was established.

The Labour Party's attitude towards organising the unemployed was half hearted and ineffectual, while many trade union leaders saw the unemployed as lying outside their traditional role of defending the employed at work. But it was a basic hostility to the CP that moulded general attitudes to the NUWM, even though at the time the CP's policy was to try and develop joint work with trade unions and other working class organisations.

A further deterioration in the relationship was precipitated when the CP changed its attitude towards the wider labour movement in the late twenties – the so called "class against class policy". This was adopted by the CP in line with the decision of the 1928 Congress of the Third Socialist International, to which it was affiliated. The Third International, dominated by the policies of Stalin, took the view that the crisis of capitalism in this period was heightening, and a revolutionary upsurge throughout the world was on the cards. Thus the parties of the Third International were to go all out in attacking the "reformist" leaders of trade unions, and other "reformist" parties, who were characterised as "social

Photo 38: The first unemployed march from Liverpool to London, 1922.

fascists" by the International. This policy has recently been described as "catastrophic in Germany"[3] and "grotesque in Britain",[4] but however we assess it now, the net effect in Britain was to push the CP into a period of fierce criticism of the TUC and the Labour Party, and both the TUC and the Labour leadership were quick to point this out as justification for their own hostile attitude towards the NUWM. The NUWM was increasingly dismissed as the "pawn of Moscow". The fact remains that by failing to take up the challenge of unemployment in the first place the Labour Party and Trade Unions left a vacuum which the CP filled. Thus when the problem of unemployment became the central issue facing the working class from 1929, it was the NUWM which provided the *only* focus for the organisation of the unemployed.

From 1929 the NUWM grew steadily. In September of that year it had forty-six branches nationwide.[5] By February 1931 it had established sixty-two branches nationally,[6] and grew rapidly in that year as the problem of unemployment grew more pressing. By October it had 277 branches,[7] and by the spring of 1932 almost 350,[8] probably the peak of its achievement. It organised national hunger marches in 1929, 1930, 1932, 1934, and finally in 1936. At a national level it also organised numerous demonstrations at Labour Party and TUC conferences. The Labour Party and the TUC ordered all local Labour Parties and Trade Councils not to give any support to the hunger marchers up to 1934, although local parties disobeyed those orders on occasions.[9] Even in 1936, the Labour Party, while not forbidding aid, "advised against" support.[10] In 1930 the NUWM was placed on the list of proscribed organisations by the Labour Party, and in a pamphlet on unemployment issued by the Labour Party in 1933 the NUWM was described as a "mere instrument of the British Communist Party".[11] The TUC for its part refused even to receive a delegation of the unemployed led by the NUWM to its 1932 conference,[12] and in December 1934 the General Council of the TUC wrote to the NUWM that it would no longer even reply to any communications.[13] Of course many Trade Unionists and members of the Labour Party worked with the NUWM at a local level, but always on an individual basis. So while the NUWM was succeeding at a national level in organising the unemployed and bringing the issue of unemployment to the forefront of political debate in the thirties, the "official" labour movement stayed resolutely hostile to its existence. In 1933 the success of the NUWM prompted the TUC to belatedly set up Unemployed Associations organised by Trades Councils to take up the issue of unemployment. These were clearly an attempt to try to rival the NUWM rather than work with it, but it says a lot for the relative strengths and weaknesses of the two organisations in working with the unemployed that in Liverpool, and in many other areas, the Unemployed Organisations could only tail behind the NUWM. Most of them eventually were absorbed into local NUWM branches.[14]

In the thirties, then, it was the NUWM that virtually alone organised the unemployed, and the history of the Hunger Marches and other national agitation on behalf of the unemployed is well known.[15] But it was also the detailed work on behalf of the unemployed in the localities that explains the strength that the NUWM was able to develop. In organising demonstrations over the level of benefits to the Boards of Guardians and Public Assistance Committees, in representing individuals over their particular cases at appeals, in defending the unemployed against evictions, in organising educational and social activities for the unemployed, and in simply being the only body that the unemployed could turn to if they wanted to fight back against their situation, the NUWM was able to build support which resulted in many minor, if unrecorded, victories, and even some major, if only temporary, successes. The history of the NUWM on Merseyside bears this out.

The NUWM on Merseyside

In the twenties and thirties the NUWM was constantly involved in a battle in support of the unemployed on Merseyside. The Liverpool, Bootle and Birkenhead branches of the movement in particular were engaged in a never-ending variety of activities ranging from individual case-work on behalf of claimants to organising local support for the hunger marches. The local branches were all affiliated to the national organisation of the NUWM, and local branches issued cards to members for a penny a week. However, the activities of the branches were open to all the ranks of the unemployed, and not just the paid up members. Inevitably as people drifted in or out of work and as different issues came to the fore at various stages of the campaign there was a high turnover of membership, so estimating the total numbers of people who were members through the thirties is impossible, let alone the numbers who may only have been involved in particular demonstrations or campaigns. The total membership nationally probably never exceeded 25,000,[16] but that figure would clearly underestimate greatly the real influence of the NUWM. Wal Hannington claimed at one point that "millions" were involved in the movement at one time or another. High turn over of membership was probably even higher on Merseyside given the casual nature of much work available in the area, but, nevertheless, the various branches were able to keep up their campaigning throughout the thirties.

What held together the branches during this difficult organisational situation were the two main strengths of the NUWM; firstly, the existence of a dedicated and increasingly experienced leadership, and, secondly, the broad degree of support that the movement was able to generate in the ranks of the unemployed at a local level. Joe Rawlings in Birkenhead, Owen Kelly in Bootle, Leo McGree in Liverpool were the leaders of the three main local branches. Aside from them, there were a large number of local organisers of the movement who carried out the mundane work of leafletting, fund raising, representing individuals at tribunals, organising social and educational activities, stewarding demonstrations and so on. It was out of this constant attention to detail that the NUWM was able to generate its local support. It was not only involved in dramatic events like the hunger marches or the Birkenhead riots of 1932. More than just a publicity campaign on behalf of the unemployed, it actually organised and worked with the unemployed.

To really appreciate the enormous range of activities of the NUWM on Merseyside we need to try to list the various types of issues that they tackled. Unfortunately the records of their activities are fragmentary: the local press gave little publicity to the NUWM, and other written sources are rare. Fortunately there are a number of people who were active in the movement in the thirties whom we were able to trace, and their oral testimony has been invaluable to us.

Organisation on Merseyside – The Organiser's View
One person who was ideally situated to get an overall view of the NUWM locally was Ted Williams, who was an organiser for the movement in the Lancashire area around the mid-thirties. This is how he remembered the situation fifty years after the event:

"For a long period I was the national organiser for the NUWM and I spent a long period travelling around the North of England organising unemployed activities and branches in West Yorkshire and North East Lancashire and parts of Cumberland. Later I became the Lancashire organiser for the NUWM. Of course, since Liverpool was the centre of the unemployed activities in Lancashire, Liverpool was the centre for the organisation of the whole area.

After the National Government election of 1931, and the Means test and the cuts in social services which occurred under that government, the unemployed activity on Merseyside took a more organised turn. The NUWM had existed since soon after the First World War. The primary organiser was Wal Hannington and he was naturally interested in organisation on Merseyside. A large contingent from Merseyside took part in the Hunger March of 1934, and following this organised activity took place on a much larger scale.

Various branches were organised in the Merseyside area. there was a branch in Birkenhead and there were two main branches in Liverpool. Their activities became increasingly directed against the idea that unemployment should be a permanent feature of society. In other words it wasn't just a question of fighting for decent standards for the unemployed, it was also a question of fighting for work, so the slogan of all our activities was "work or full maintenance". The branches were organised in the inner city areas in the localities, they were part of neighbourhoods. It was easy at a time of empty shops in the slum areas to take a shop at a low rent, where we'd organise a group to form a branch of the NUWM. In other areas where this wasn't possible, such as housing estates and so on, the people used to meet in each other's houses. But it was a grassroots organisation.

The local branches had meetings almost every night of the week all over the area. There was always a strong branch of the movement in Bootle, particularly in the Marsh Lane area, and their activities, because the local paper was a small paper, did get more publicity from the press than we got in Liverpool. Generally the press played down our activities unless something very startling happened, nor were we ever given the facilities as are given now by the BBC and the rest of the media. There was a conspiracy of silence and this is why the importance of the NUWM is not recognised by some of our so-called historians. the activity took place daily, everybody knew about it by word of mouth, everybody knew about the demonstrations, everybody knew when victories were gained, because we did gain victories by stopping cuts, and sometimes by getting increases. It was the activity of the NUWM which forced the Tory National Government to insert a clause in the National Assistance regulations which was known colloquially as the "pots and pans clause" which enabled somebody drawing unemployment benefit to make a claim for extra money to buy necessities for the house which deteriorated during a period of unemployment. This is just one example of the kinds of things that were only possible because of the organisation of the unemployed by the NUWM.

When a branch was formed it was noticeable what latent talents there were among the unemployed, what could be done by volunteers in a short space of time, in collecting buckshee timber as they used to call it, in knocking up a few tables, knocking up a desk for me in this little office in Paddington. The enthusiasm and intelligence of these people proved what was being wasted by mass unemployment. Of course these activities had an educational value, because politics were being discussed seriously, and not on a a shallow level as happens in the press and at that time in most political parties.

The subscription was only a penny a week and most of the money came from collections at meetings, and of course occasionally in a branch we were able to have a billiard table and make a few bob to pay the rent of the shop we were using as branch headquarters. There was a strong branch in Scotland Road and a strong branch in Paddington. These were both areas of mass unemployment, bad housing and poverty.

The criticism has been made that it was a communist organisation. Well in a sense there were very often active Communists connected with the unemployed workers movement. But the majority of the unemployed had been apolitical, rather disinterested, and most of our members came from people who'd taken no part in politics before. We had a lot of ex-servicemen who had fought for "homes fit for heroes" to live in, who'd been unemployed for a long period, and on our marches many of them wore their war medals. These people were particularly active in the movement for the obvious reason that the grandiose promises given to them when they went to the Great War had not been fulfilled. We had a large number of youngsters who couldn't get work at all or who hadn't worked. They were the brighter types who had begun to think for themselves because of economic conditions. And these people had a place to go to, instead of hanging round street corners or vegetating at home, they had a branch to go to, they could talk, have a game of billiards, some branches had a game of table tennis, they took part in chalking the streets, an activity, something useful to do.

The NUWM was a completely democratic organisation. The branches elected their own representatives to National Conference, which was held every year, and the National Administrative Council which ran the movement on a day to day basis was elected at the conference and represented every area in the country where branches existed. Wal Hannington and everybody else depended for their position on the support and the votes of all the members. There were frequent bulletins from the head office in London keeping the branches up to date with any developments and the activities of the movement all over the country, and the information was available to all members. There was nothing hidden, either in terms of finance, organisation, membership or anything else."[17]

Organisation on Merseyside – The Rank and File View

Another person who remembers well the activities of the NUWM is George Hughes, who was involved in a short lived branch of the movement in the South End of Liverpool in the mid-thirties. This is his testimony:

"Somewhere around about '35, between '35 and '36, we set up a branch of the NUWM in Park Road. It was known as the South branch. It actually was formed by, or shall we say the convenor was a bloke called Ted Williams, who at the time was a well known member of the Communist Party. You couldn't form a branch of the CP in the particular area I lived in because it was predominantly Tory, only by virtue of religion.

Anyway we got some premises in Park Road, I don't know where we got the money from or what happened, I think we were actually subsidised by maybe the CP or the Labour Party for that matter, we don't know. However, this Ted Williams came down and he got us all in the room in the club on these premises and we started forming committees, you know, we had to have a secretary and all this. Your know we weren't sure about this thing, we'd never been formed together as a body, we just stuck together as a crowd of unemployed people, which we all were obviously.

For some reason I was a member of the Services Committee, at the time to me that sounded like the army, but I didn't realize what it was until later on. Having said that, from nowhere we got a billiard table given to us which we set up on the ground floor, and then we had a canteen upstairs and dartboards and a few indoor games, which more or less was great in a way because at the time I was on the dock and there was no work, so when you signed on, in the morning when you looked around for work, afterwards we used to pass away our time in there.

When we started we had about twenty or thirty. The membership built up in a couple of weeks once they got the billiard table in and the games room and a cup of tea for a ha'penny. You used to pay a ha'penny for a cup of tea – I used to look after the canteen when I was off – and it built up and built up a penny a week I think was the subs. I think the billiards was a penny or twopence a game, it paid the rent of course it was very low in those days. It built up because it became a social club.

I remember the room being full with twenty or thirty at the start, and there were that many committees everyone was on a committee of some sort. There were all sorts of committees, well we had a finance committee, an entertainments committee, a services committee, canteen committee, social committee, political committee. We had political discussions. We attended meetings, we attended rallies. I think once we sent some representatives over to Birkenhead.

With regard to the services committee, I remember an African coming in and he'd been up to what we called in those days the Parish, and they'd refused him, people used to send them to us. Then I was told, being a member of the services committee and the only one available, I would have to go up with him and confront this man, and his name I'll remember as long as I live, Mr Phythian, he was one bad man for the people round here, he was in charge of that parish and he'd give nobody nothing. There was always a policeman on duty, always in every one of those offices in those days, and I remember going up with this African, and as we walked in the door, you know, service committee, NUWM badge and everything, this policeman said "where are you going?", and promptly threw the two of us out. No messing, "come in here again", he said, "and I'll do you", you know, no messing, he threatened to kill you and all this, and I went back with my tail between my legs. I think I resigned off the services committee.

Another time, I don't know what happened but we got a load of instruments, we got a couple of drums, a big drum, a mace and about ten flutes given to us. So there was an organised march of the NUWM, all the NUWM were to meet at Edge Hill lamp, and Bessie Braddock was one of the main speakers. So we formed up in Park Road outside the club, and this is the funny bit, there was nobody could play any of these instruments, there was only one bloke could play the kettle drum, one bloke could play the big drum, and one bloke named Beech Keighly who was very well known in the South End, could play the flute. But we all took an instrument and we all marched to Edge Hill lamp. We were going "ph, ph, ph, ..." noiselessly, really there was only two players and the drum, and Tommy Devlin was leading us in the front with this stick. Well when we got to Edge Hill lamp the mounted police were there and the ordinary police were there, and the next minute there's absolute mayhem...they didn't care for life or limb them police, the horses just run at you and that was it...Needless to say that smashed all that lot up. But these were the sorts of things that used to happen.

We used to have meetings, the meetings were quite good, what we were going to do and what we weren't going to do, but nothing ever came of it because we just weren't strong enough. The word got round that this NUWM was just a front for the CP. As time went on it just lapsed into a social club, it didn't get off the ground up here like it did in Bootle or Birkenhead. Maybe it wasn't allowed to get off the ground in the area we lived in.

Anyway we just carried on, and then people were just coming in and joining it, it became a social club. It was infiltrated by different people. The next thing I knew was I went to go there one morning after signing on, I wasn't in the night before, and the whole place was wrecked completely, billiard table smashed up, just absolutely destroyed, windows broken, everything. And Bill Grey who was the secretary, a smashing bloke, they'd worked out on him, you know, there was all sorts of fellows beat up on both sides. But no action was taken by the police, they weren't interested. the idea was, let them kill each other, why should we worry. This business of the police running in to stop riots and all that was ridiculous, they did it if they had horses and there was about 200 of them to about five of you was their attitude.

We only lasted a couple of months, I mean we went back then to listening to Leo McGree, he was our idol, he was really one good man that man, he was really working class from head to foot, and he was the only commie that we knew really, and we followed him, we liked him, and we always picked up on his jargon and all that.

Then in '36, '37, things began to brighten up a bit, well as far as I'm concerned they did."[18]

These, then, are some of the memories of the NUWM locally of people who were involved at the time. But what were the campaigns and the issues which the NUWM was concerned with once a branch had been established?

Individual Case Work

The rock on which the NUWM built its support among the unemployed was the help and advice on benefits that it offered to individuals. Coping with the various relief bodies and ensuring that you got the benefit you were entitled to was an intimidating and complicated process. Wal Hannington explained the procedure that people had to go through in defending themselves before courts of referees under the genuinely seeking work clause;

"The onus of proof under examination by a court of referees rested upon the claimant, who had to prove that he was genuinely seeking work ... unemployed applicants before the court would find themselves subjected to a rapid fire of questions about the places to which they had applied for employment ... Many unemployed workers entered the courts in fear and trembling, knowing that the meagre labour exchange benefit for themselves and their family was in the balance. Trick questions were often put to the applicants in an effort to secure a contradiction of some previous statement, and under a gruelling cross-examination the applicant often lost his nerve and was unable to remember important points in his search for work which would have helped him to avoid disqualification."[19]

NUWM branches spent much of their time aiding individual claimants trying to secure their benefit. They picketed the dole queues and handed out leaflets explaining the regulations and advised applicants before appeals and tribunals. They were the only body in existence that was able to offer this aid to the unemployed. Over the years the NUWM built up a considerable amount of expertise in these cases. Harry McShane recounted:

"Every branch had its own committee to distribute duties among its members. People were appointed to specific tasks, including fighting cases at the labour exchange and the Public Assistance Committee. Some NUWM members became very well acquainted with the unemployment insurance regulations and the public assistance rules. They collected all the literature on the regulations, and every case they fought provided more experience."[20]

Another national leader of the NUWM, Sid Elias, explained the rationale behind the emphasis that the movement put on this kind of work as follows:

"... during the time I was with the NUWM I was insisting on the representation of unemployed people ... the representation of people knowing their rights. I published three handbooks, I didn't publish them myself, the NUWM, but I drafted them 'The Easy Guide to the Unemployed Insurance Act' and that's what they were, they sold in the thousands they were only a penny a copy, didn't matter where you went to speak you could sell thousands of these because they'd just grab at them. I also insisted on taking the cases up with the insurance authorities ... well I mean if you get a man his benefit well surely that's something, and if you train them how to handle themselves in front of Courts of Referees and things of this kind it all helps. You'd be greater in their estimation than just banging words at them, revolutionary slogans and things of that kind ..."[21]

This then was the bread and butter work of the NUWM on Merseyside as in the rest of the country. It didn't hit the headlines, but it won the movement widespread support among the unemployed. Frank Deegan, a leading member of the Bootle branch recalled that:

"Hardly a day went by without us engaging in some form of activity. Often we had to defend individuals who were being harshly or unfairly treated by officials of the relief and the assistance organisations."[22]

George Hughes' experience of this kind of work when he was a member of the "services committee" of his branch was not so successful, as we saw earlier, but in numerous cases the aid of the NUWM helped individuals get the claim that they were entitled to. For them it was a small victory against an imposing and hostile bureaucracy. Ted Williams also stresses that this work was essential in gaining the support of the unemployed for the movement:

"In those days most of the unemployed in Liverpool had exhausted their unemployment benefits and were living on public assistance, or outdoor relief, so that there was a constant struggle with the local PAC. This involved representing the people, putting their case at these committee meetings and fighting tooth and nail for as much as possible for these people. This activity was taking place all the time. In addition to that, the NUWM had by some strange quirk been recognised in the twenties as an association of employed workers, and was therefore able to represent people who were drawing unemployment when they went to the Courts of Referees or other tribunals connected with the Ministry of Labour. These activities were taking place continually, and were more important in building up organisation and branches than the actual meetings and demonstrations that were taking place all the time, important though these were."[23]

The Struggle Over Housing

The NUWM also played a vital role in the sphere of the housing and rents of the unemployed. Ted Williams recalls:

"Another activity of course occurred when there was an attempt at an eviction, because it was extremely difficult for people to buy food never mind pay rent. In these cases a squad would leave the local branch and go into the house ready to resist the bailiffs with suitable banners outside advertising what they were doing, and invariably the bailiffs failed to appear. The feeling in the area as a result of the agitation made the landlord and the authorities think twice about these things. Again this was the important thing about the NUWM that it was a grass-roots organisation."[24]

Frank Deegan also recalled that:

"Our activities were not confined to leading the struggle for work or increased benefits. We defended workers who, through no fault of their own, were under threats of eviction from their homes. About twenty members of the Bootle branch of the NUWM went to the assistance of a family with six young children who were in immediate danger of losing their home. My pals, with the consent of the parents, entered the house to try to prevent the bailiffs getting in. The police arrived ... eventually the cops forced their way in...my

Photo 39: NUWM-led resistance to an eviction of an unemployed family in Dagenham in November 1932 is finally ended by a violent police attack. Such resistance to evictions also took place in Liverpool under the leadership of the NUWM.

elder brother was one of those arrested. They were charged with forcible entry, obstructing the bailiffs ... and obstructing the police ... They were all heavily fined, which we managed to pay through collections."[25]

Another example of this kind of activity to defend the unemployed against eviction was recorded in the *Daily Post* in August 1935.[26] NUWM members went to the house of an unemployed man threatened with eviction in Bootle. They advised him on his legal rights, and when the bailiffs arrived inspected the warrant and established that it was not legal. After the bailiffs had started with the eviction, a crowd of 400 who had gathered outside marched with the tenant to the offices of the landlord in Brasenose Road. The tenant demanded to see the landlord, but before he had appeared the police arrived and the tenant was arrested and charged with a breach of the peace. The crowd then marched back to his house on Second Street and proceeded to put the furniture back in the house.

A further case of such activity in Bootle was described as the "unemployed fighting day" in the pages of the *Daily Worker* in February 1932.[27] An unemployed worker in South Drive had been evicted, but a group of NUWM members installed him back in his house, along with his furniture which had been put in the street. They then barricaded themselves in the house and hoisted a red flag from one of the upper windows. By this time a large crowd had assembled outside the house, and when the police arrived and attempted to break into the house fierce fighting broke out, as a result of which twenty-one of the demonstrators were arrested. Another case later that year involved the eviction of an eighty-two year old man from a house in Montague Street.[28] A crowd of over 1,000 had gathered outside the house and held up traffic before the bailiffs had arrived to carry out the County Court order. After the bailiffs had carried out the tenant's furniture and placed it on a cart, a group of NUWM members intervened and replaced the furniture, at the same time forcing the bailiffs to leave the scene in disarray.

The NUWM also tackled other housing questions on behalf of the unemployed. Harry Mcshane records that the movement made use of the Rent Restrictions Act of 1915, one clause of which stated that rent could be reduced if repairs were not done. By forcing the implementation of this Act in individual cases the NUWM was able to get rents reduced for the unemployed, sometimes to almost nothing where housing conditions were particularly bad.[29] The Liverpool branch of the NUWM took up this issue over Corporation housing in September 1935. The *Daily Post* reported that the NUWM called a mass meeting of 600 people in Edgar Street to protest against the Estates Committee charging tenants rent for property that had been declared unfit for human habitation, and supporting Labour members of the Council in trying to get this policy changed.[30] In October the NUWM also sent a deputation to the PAC demanding that rent should not be paid for houses declared unfit, and also demanding that there should be no deduction from relief for applicants who succeeded in getting their rents lawfully reduced for this reason.[31]

Local Agitation Over Benefits

The third major area of work that the NUWM was involved in at a local level was in fighting for improvements in the level of benefits, and better treatment of the unemployed by the relief authorities. The struggle against the Means Test, the genuinely seeking work clause, the Anomalies Act, the cuts in benefit carried out in 1927, 1931, and 1935, the variations in benefits allowed by BOGS and PACs were constantly fought by the NUWM through mass meetings, demonstrations, deputations to relief bodies and Council meetings. Sometimes these activities escalated into riots, most notably in 1932 in Birkenhead and Liverpool, as police harassment of these activities was unremitting. Few NUWM activists on Merseyside avoided a spell inside sometime in the thirties. Nevertheless, the chalking of the streets to advertise meetings (it was illegal to chalk the walls, so the streets became the notice boards of the NUWM) continued through the thirties. As we shall see these forms of direct action at times produced results. Cuts were sometimes restored as a result of NUWM pressure, extra allowances were sometimes won, PACs were forced to raise benefit to come into line with neighbouring Committees.

The earliest example of the NUWM's participation in direct action of this sort on Merseyside was in 1927 following the cuts in Unemployment Benefit and Poor Relief introduced nationally. Numerous demonstrations were organised in Merseyside by the NUWM to protest at these cuts. After the West Derby Board of Guardians had reduced relief by 1s. and imposed more stringent conditions on who should qualify for relief in September 1927, the NUWM organised a demonstration outside the meeting of the Board in November. The Guardians refused to see a deputation from the NUWM, which resulted in "an unruly scene" according to the *Daily Post*, and Labour members of the Board were expelled from the meeting by the police.[32] At the next meeting of the Board in February 1928 a demonstration was organised, and the Guardians agreed to see a deputation from the crowd. The deputation put the case for an increase in relief, but a motion to that effect was subsequently defeated.[33] In this particular case the NUWM pressure was ineffective, but elsewhere on Merseyside they made temporary gains. The Birkenhead Guardians raised some of their scales of relief in January 1928 and relaxed their qualification rules, although this led to pressure from the Ministry of Health which eventually resulted in a cut in outdoor relief rates in June 1928.[34]

This sort of pressure by the NUWM on the various relief bodies was carried on relentlessly through the thirties, with varying degrees of success. In September 1932 the agitation against the Means Test and cuts in benefit instituted by the PAC's on both sides of the river resulted in the riots documented in Chapter 6. It also forced the Birkenhead PAC to raise the rates of relief and also institute some public works schemes to provide work for the unemployed. A local victory perhaps, but a victory nevertheless.

In 1934 the local branches of the NUWM in Bootle, Birkenhead, and Liverpool mounted a concerted campaign over the level of unemployed rates. They led delegations to the Bootle PAC in September, Birkenhead in November, and Liverpool in December, and they eventually succeeded in winning a general raising of the rates in Bootle in January 1935, and a minor victory in Birkenhead with the raising of child allowance and coal and rent allowances.[35]

Again in 1935 resistance to the operation of the new Unemployed Assistance Board and the associated cuts in benefit was co-ordinated by the NUWM. In February, marches were organised by the three main branches on Merseyside in Bootle, Birkenhead, and Liverpool, followed by a rally on 4th March in the stadium which also received support from the local Trades Council and Labour Party for the first time: The Liverpool Trades Council and Labour Party supported the rally, and local Labour Party figures including Logan and Bessie Braddock spoke on the platform. On the same day the Bootle Trades Council and Labour Party and the Bootle branch of the NUWM organised a march to North Park.[36]

This campaign was reflected across the whole country by other branches of the movement, and represented perhaps the highest point of the NUWM in its ability to coordinate national activity on behalf of the unemployed. It was also probably the single most important victory won by the NUWM, because it forced the government into passing the "Standstill Act".

The Hunger Marches

Of course all the local work of the NUWM was backed up by the most famous manifestation of the movement, the national hunger marches, and on Merseyside as in the rest of the country the local branches worked tirelessly in building up support for the marches. There was always a group from Merseyside on all the marches, going back to the first national march in 1922/3, which had a contingent of Liverpool dockers and seamen on it. For the marches in 1934 and 1936 in particular major campaigns of support were mounted. Street collections, public meetings, motions to union branches calling for support were organised by the NUWM, with increasing success. The Bootle branch alone was able to finance twenty marchers in 1934, and forty in 1936, and the dockers' section of the Transport and General Workers' Union was persuaded to send three members on the 1934 march and donate 30s each for them. In 1934 a large crowd saw off the march from Liverpool, brandishing banners saying "Remember Birkenhead" and "Remember Belfast" (an echo of the riots in 1932), and again in 1936 the Liverpool contingent received a huge send off.

The attitude of the Labour Party nationally to the marches was reflected as well on Merseyside. Simon Mahon's condemnation of the NUWM quoted earlier was not untypical, and only limited sections of the Labour Party on Merseyside ever gave belated support, as Ted Williams relates:

"I've often been amazed that in a town like Liverpool where there was such terrible poverty, awful slums, squalor, no possible hope it seemed of any kind of economic recovery, the slight recovery that was taking place elsewhere certainly did not affect Liverpool, that the local Labour Party and Trade Unions were so indifferent to the unemployed. In fact it did seem at times that apart from a few Trade Union branches where there were some left wingers in official posts, they were completely indifferent to the unemployed. I heard one Labour Councillor actually suggesting that they should not take part in a demonstration against the Tory Party's attempts to cut outdoor relief for the unemployed, and he himself was a member of the PAC.

Photos 40 & 41: (40) Above: The women's section of the 1932 hunger march passing through Luton. The woman in the second row with the scarf was the youngest marcher, aged sixteen, and from Liverpool. (41) Opposite: Two members of the 1932 march outside Holloway Prison following their arrest during the disturbances at Hyde Park. On the right, Miss O'Rourke, the sixteen year old from Liverpool, and still smiling.

Photo 41

197

Photo 42: The Liverpool contingent of 200 to the 1936 hunger march set off down Lord Street.

Locally the Labour Party and the Trades Council were either indifferent or hostile. The only change occurred around 1935 and 1936 when the St. Anne's ward, the Labour Party there participated actively in the unemployed activities, Bessie Braddock, Davey Nickson, J.D. Mack and Jack Braddock himself were the only local Labour people of note who participated in these activities. The activities of this Labour group were very valuable in that we had liaison with the police and local Municipal departments. There were really magnificent demonstrations which took place in the courtyard of a big block of working class flats in the St. Anne's area which we christened "Unity Square", I think its actually called St. Anne's Square. There were numerous huge demonstrations there in which the NUWM and Braddock and the others participated."[37]

Even this support was condemned by the hierarchy of the local labour movement. In May 1936 Bessie Braddock publicly criticised the Labour Party candidate for the Abercromby ward of the city, a Mrs. Elliot, for her lack of sympathy towards applicants to the PAC. For this Bessie Braddock was censured by the Trades Council and Labour Party. Again in March 1938 she was censured for speaking on the same platform as a NUWM speaker.[38]

The hunger marches are well documented elsewhere, but we need to stress that these powerful symbols of the distress and anger of the unemployed were built on the day to day work of the NUWM. The Labour Party and Trade Unions gave little or no support to them until popular feeling behind the marchers forced them to jump on the bandwagon. In the end the power of the marches depended on the support which the NUWM had deservedly won. The image still echoes today:

> Ten thousand of the desperate marching by,
> Five foot, six foot, seven foot high.[39]

Notes

1. *Liverpool Daily Post*, 24.1.1935.
2. W. Hannington, *Unemployed Struggles 1919-36* (London, Lawrence & Wishart, 1977), pp.322-3.
3. R. Miliband, *Parliamentary Socialism* (London, Allen & Unwin, 1961), p.217.
4. Ibid, p.217.
5. *Report of Sixth National Conference of the NUWM*, Sept. 14-16, 1929.
6. *Report of Seventh National Conference of the NUWM*, Feb. 21-23, 1931.
7. National Administrative Committee, NUWM, *Minutes*, Jan. 23-24, 1932.
8. NAC, *Minutes*, May 7-8, 1932.
9. P. Kingsford, *The Hunger Marches in Britain 1920-40* (London, Lawrence & Wishart, 1982), p.168.
10. Ibid, p.201.
11. Ibid, pp.165-68.
12. Ibid, p.138

13. *Daily Worker*, 21.12.1934.
14. J. Lovell & B.C. Roberts, *A Short History of the TUC* (London, Macmillan, 1968), p.129; Kingsford, p.168.
15. For details of the Hunger Marches, see Kingsford, Hannington.
16. S. Davies, 'The Membership of the national Unemployed Workers' Movement, 1923-1938', *Labour History Review*, Vol. 57, No.1 May 1992.
17. Interview with Ted Williams, 7.9.1983.
18. Interview with George Hughes, 23.9.1983.
19. Hannington, p.180.
20. H. McShane, *No Mean Fighter* (London, Pluto, 1978), p.185.
21. "The Reminiscences of Sid Elias", *Bulletin of the Society for the Study of Labour History*, Spring 1979.
22. F. Deegan, *There's No Other Way* (Liverpool, Toulouse Press, 1980), p.20.
23. Ted Williams.
24. Ibid.
25. Deegan, p.16.
26. *Liverpool Daily Post*, 21.8.1935.
27. *Daily Worker*, 25.2.1932.
28. Ibid, 4.8.1932.
29. McShane, p.205.
30. *Liverpool Daily Post*, 12.9.1935.
31. Ibid, *10.10.1935*.
32. Ibid, 24.11.1927.
33. Ibid, 2.2.1928.
34. See Chapter 5, p.??.
35. *Liverpool Daily Post*, 15.9.1934; 27.11.1934; 20.12.1934; 24.1.1935.
36. Ibid, 22.2.1935; 25.2.1935; 4.3.1935.
37. Ted Williams.
38. *Liverpool Daily Post*, 12.3.1938
39. Quoted in A. Kettle, 'W.H. Auden: Poetry and Politics in the Thirties', *Culture and Crisis in Britain in the 30s*, (ed.) J. Clark, M. Heinemann, D. Margolies & C. Snee (London, Lawrence & Wishart, 1979).

POSTSCRIPT

"I was 19 in 1961, my father was 54, and my grandfather about 75. In a once-in-a-lifetime fit of confidence brought on, as I recall, by my A level results which had obviously lofted me into the lap of perpetual security, my father told me, 'We'll never see mass unemployment again – the bosses are afraid of it, the Government wouldn't allow it, and anyway the workers just wouldn't take it.'

'Wrong,' said my grandfather. 'The bosses can't do without it, the Government depends on the bosses and as long as it happens nice and gradual the workers won't even notice until it's too late.'

'Well,' said my grandmother, 'even if our boy did have to go on the dole for a bit, they'd look after him and his family now – not like before.'

'And that's the best thing,' said my mother, 'the youngsters don't have to feel frightened like we did.'"

Thirty years on, and the young 'A' level man from that typically proud and supportive Welsh working class family had graduated to become the leader of Her Majesty's Opposition. Thirty years on and the warnings of his sage old grandfather have tragically materialised. Millions, including hundred of thousands of youngsters, are experiencing the same fears as their great-grandparents had in the hungry thirties. Is Kinnock's an exaggerated, if unpleasantly familiar, 'family' history? As we move into the second consecutive decade of mass unemployment, the answer must be emphatically, "no". Nevertheless, his strong sense of *deja vu* is of itself not enough in dealing with "the one absolute evil" which links and obligates our generation to that of his grandparents. That is going to require a political will and determination to solve unemployment, conspicuously lacking to date. The "battle against unemployment" has to be made the number one priority of Government in order to prevent a perpetuation of waste which so obviously afflicted millions in the thirties.

In this book we have tried to describe the experience of mass unemployment sixty years ago on Merseyside. We have done so for two main reasons. First, because that experience had until very recently been forgotten and distorted. Second, because we are now going through a period when history appears to be repeating itself. We have avoided stressing comparisons between "then and now", preferring to let readers make their own conclusions. But some of the implications of our study should be emphasised.

Myth and Reality: From the "Devil's Decade" to "Recovery on the Dole"

It is necessary to question the conclusions that have been reached by some revisionist historians of the inter-war period, and their subtle reinterpretation of the thirties in particular. The pessimist view of widespread social distress and human waste in the thirties has given way (but decidedly not in this book) to a much more optimistic picture of 'bright spots' and new jobs in clean new industries, improvements in health and housing, wider access to consumer good and so on. Instead of the portrayal of the thirties as a disastrous decade, the optimists emphasise the strength and vigour of "recovery on the dole". As Conservative politicians pointed to the supposed "economic miracle" of the late nineteen-eighties and the gap between illusion and reality widened, that sickeningly ironic phrase for the thirties was seen to have its practical uses, at least until the present (now officially defined) 'recession' set in.

We argue that no amount of rewriting history can disguise the fact that the experience of mass unemployment was one of disaster and waste for both the unemployed and those in work. These were unequivocally desperate times. The memories of hunger marchers and the means test are incomplete without reference to the experiences of rationalisation and speed up. The "baronial supervision" of factory foremen in non-unionised firms, and the insidious threat of the sack and long dole queues served to keep the employed in line.

The Myth of the Wigan Miner

In a rather different way the experience of the thirties has been distorted in public memory by certain key images. The picture of the Wigan miner in Chapter 2 has become justifiably famous in encapsulating the misery of unemployment in the thirties. It is an image which is incomplete and potentially misleading. The northern, male, industrial worker is seen as the archetypical victim of the decade. We have seen, however, that the misery was spread much more widely than that. The woman worker, the young, workers in new industries and new housing estates, black workers, all of these were also the victims of mass unemployment in the thirties.

"They Were Starving, But They Didn't Riot"

Another myth about the thirties became highly significant in the politics of the nineteen-eighties: that the working class was apathetic, demoralised and inactive in the face of the misery of mass unemployment. In its most condescending and politically malicious form, the myth is that the unemployed bore their hardship with quiet docility. Margaret Thatcher and Norman Tebbit among others plugged this particular lie assiduously as a handy weapon with which to castigate the unemployed of the eighties. "In the thirties," they said, "people were unemployed but they didn't riot, they got on their bikes and looked for work." When on the evening of 3 July 1981 violence erupted in the Toxteth Riots, many seventy year olds on Merseyside would have remembered that those on the dole in Birkenhead had taken the same decisive action in the autumn of 1932. The unemployed *did* riot and fight back, as Mosley found out to his cost when he visited Liverpool in 1936. However unfavourable the economic and political climate was for the working class, they still struggled against the system that oppressed them. They struggled against the means test and the cuts in benefit through the NUWM; they fought for the right to join a union to defend themselves at work; they struggled against the fascism of the BUF; they demonstrated against the fascism of Franco, and some even died in that struggle in the International Brigades.

The TINA Syndrome

The familiar Thatcherite slogan – "there is no alternative" – is in fact an echo of the thirties, when a similar economic fatalism was a way for governments to abdicate their responsibility for the unemployed. The emphasis on the gold standard, the grip of orthodoxy and neo-classical economics, was such that more attention was paid to prices and exchange rates than the real economic variables of output and employment.

Passive measures for the relief of the unemployed went alongside a search for economies in its provision. Those who claimed unemployed benefit had their claims rigorously scrutinised in an era renowned for strict enforcement of the "genuinely seeking work" clause and the means test. Although the latter remained in force throughout the thirties, the second Labour Government did at least abolish the "genuinely seeking work" test. In 1930 William Beveridge wrote optimistically of its demise:

Photo 43: January 1939, and only months away from war, and the unemployed are still demonstrating. Here the NUWM protest at the Prime Minister, Neville Chamberlain, leaving for discussions with Mussolini in Italy. A mounted police charge led to several protestors being arrested. The decade ends as it started.

"The condition will not, it may be hoped, ever rise from its dishonoured grave."

Sixty years on, with a slight change in nomenclature, but the same meanness of spirit and resources, that condition has indeed been seen to rise again. The "actively seeking employment" clause was an integral part of the 1989 Social Security Bill and the renewed efforts to cut the benefit of the unemployed. As *The New Statesman and Society* asked of the measure,

"How many letters or telephone calls per week will be required? How many newspaper adverts will claimants be expected to scan? What allowances will be made for reading or language difficulties, or for the hopelessness that results from months of fruitless job-hunting?"

Now it may be telephone calls rather than the wearing out of leather soles in the soul-destroying search for work, but so many have been there before.

One final thought springs to mind as we reflect on the thirties – it is the sheer waste and futility of it all. As the Macmillan Committee asked in 1931:

"If we can do what we are doing with nearly a quarter of our industrial resources idle, what might we not do if they were all employed?"

In 1992 the question is still waiting to be answered.

Recommended Reading

This is not a comprehensive bibliography, but rather a guide to some of the more accessible sources for the general reader. Most of these books should be available in local libraries if they are not to be found in book-shops.

General Works

S. Glynn and J. Oxborrow, *Interwar Britain: A Social and Economic History*, (London, 1976).

C.L. Mowatt, *Britain Between the Wars, 1918-40*, (London, 2nd edition, 1968).

General Works on Merseyside History

J. Belchem (ed.), *Popular Politics, Riot and Labour: Essays in Liverpool History, 1790-1940* (Liverpool, 1992).

L.W. Brady, *T.P. O'Connor and the Liverpool Irish*, (London, 1983).

H.R. Hikins (ed.), *Building the Union: Studies on the Growth of the Workers' Movement: Merseyside, 1756-1967*, (Liverpool, 1973).

Tony Lane, *Liverpool: Gateway of Empire*, (London, 1987).

Merseyside Social Research Group, *Merseyside in Crisis*, (Liverpool, 1980).

On the Inter-war Economy and Unemployment

D.H. Aldcroft, *The Inter-war Economy: Britain, 1919-39*, (London, 1970).

D.H. Aldcroft & H.W. Richardson, *The British Economy 1870-1939*, (London, 1969).

N. Branson and M. Heinemann, *Britain in the Nineteen Thirties* (London, 1971).

D. Caradog Jones, *Social Survey of Merseyside*, (Liverpool, 1934).

S. Constantine, *Unemployment in Britain Between the Wars* , (Harlow, 1980).

W. Hannington, *The Problem of the Distressed Areas*, (Wakefield, 1976).

C. Littler, *The Development of the Labour Process in Capitalist Society*, (London, 1982).

S. Pollard, *The Development of the British Economy, 1914-1950*, (London, 1962).

S. Pollard, *The Gold Standard and Employment Policies Between the Wars*, (London, 1970).

J. Stevenson and C. Cook, *The Slump*, (London, Jonathan Cape, 1977).

On Health, Housing and Social Conditions Between the Wars

J. Burnett, *A Social History of Housing, 1815-1970*, (London, 1978).

I. Law, *History of Race and Racism in Liverpool*, (Liverpool, 1981).

J. Lewis, *The Politics of Motherhood: child and Maternal Welfare in England 1900-1939*, (1980).

George Orwell, *The Road to Wigan Pier*, (London, 1973).

C.G. Pooley and S. Irish, *The Development of Corporation Housing in Liverpool, 1869-1945*, (Lancaster, 1984).

J. Stevenson, *British Society, 1914-45*, (Harmondsworth, 1984).

M. Swenarton, *Homes fit for Heroes: The Politics and Architecture of Early State Housing in Britain*, (London, 1981).

On Policing

M. Brogden, *The Police: Autonomy and Consent*, (London, 1982).

On the Ruling Class and Reactionary Politics

R. Benewick, *The Fascist Movement in Britain*, (London, 2nd edition, 1972).

W.D. Rubenstein, *Men of Property: The Very Wealthy in Britain Since the Industrial Revolution*, (London, 1981).

R. Skidelsky, *Oswald Mosley*, (London, 1975).

A. Thorpe (ed.), *The Failure of Political Extremism in Inter-War Britain*, (Exeter, 1989).

P.J. Waller, *Democracy and Sectarianism: A Political and Social History of Liverpool 1868-1939*, (Liverpool, 1981).

On Trade Unions and the Labour Party

A. Briggs and J. Saville (eds.), *Essays on Labour History, 1918-39*, (London, 1977).

G. Brown, *Sabotage*, (Nottingham, 1977).

K. Burgess, *The Challenge of Labour*, (London, 1980).

D. Coates, *The Labour Party and the Struggle for Socialism*, (Cambridge, 1975).

J. Hinton, *Labour and Socialism: A History of the British Labour Movement 1867-1974*, (Brighton, 1983).

K. Laybourn, *The Rise of Labour: The British Labour Party, 1890-1979*, (London, 1988).

J. Lovell and B.C. Roberts, *A Short History of the TUC*, (London, 1968).

R. Miliband, *Parliamentary Socialism*, (London, 1961).

N.C. Soldon, *Women in British Trade Unions, 1874-1976*, (Dublin, 1978).

On the NUWM and Unemployed Struggles

R. Crocher, *We Refuse to Starve in Silence: A History of the National Unemployed Workers' Movement*, (London, 1987).

F. Deegan, *There's No Other Way*, (Liverpool, 1980).

W. Hannington, *Unemployed Struggles 1919-36*, (London, 1977).

P. Kingsford, *The Hunger Marches in Britain 1920-40*, (London, 1982).

H. McShane, *No Mean Fighter*, (London, 1978).

INDEX

80, 146, 147, 153, 158, 160
National Minority Movement,
136, 180
National Unemployed Workers
Movement (NUWM) 46, 63, 72,
76, 81, 89, 98f, 104, 136-7, 158-9,
161, 177f, 203-4
 – Birkenhead Branch, 183
 – Bootle Branch, 177-8, 183
 – First National Conference, 179
 – Joint Advisory Committee
 (with TUC), 180
 – Membership, 182, 183
 – Merseyside, 183f
 – Opposition to Evictions, 190-2
 – South End Branch 186-8
National Union of Distributive and
Allied Workers (NUDAW), 134,
142
National Union of General and
Municipal Workers (NUGMW),
128, 134, 142
National Union of Police Officers,
92
Netherfield Road, 167
Netherfield Ward, 166
"New" Industries, 133
New Statesman and Society, 205
New Technology, 125f
Newman, Sir George, 42
Norris Green, 52,63

O
O'Connor, T.P., 149
"One-in-six" Rule, 68, 70
Orangeism, 148, 163f
Orwell, George, 35
Otterspool Promenade, 83
Out of Work, 179

P
Parliamentary Democracy, 146
"PC5", 157
Phillips, Marion, 77
Pier Head, 19
Pilgrim Trust, 36
Pitt St. 95
Policing, 92f,
 – BUF, 169
 – Youth, 97f
Poor Laws, 66,74
Poplar, 179
Poverty, 33
Preston, 138
Princes' Park Ward, 113, 155
Profitibility, 10
Protestant Party, 166
Protestant Reformed Church, 167
Protestant Reformer, 167
Protestant Times, 168
Protestantism, 164f
Public Assistance Committee, 66,
74, 80f, 88, 95, 99, 158
Public Sector Spending, 146

Q
Queens Drive, Walton, 173-5

R
Rathbone,Eleanor, 52
Rationalisation, 10, 20f, 40, 118f,
136-7
Rawlings, Joe, 184
Reformism, 180
Regan,Billy, 22
Restructing,economic, 12,20

Reynolds, Sir James, 168
Richardson, Fred, 154
Riots, Belfast (1932), 195

Birkenhead, see Birkenhead
Liverpool, 203
– 1919 Race Riots, 28, 167
– 1932, 102, 178, 193
– 1981, 102, 203
Robinson,Billy, 60
Roxby,Prof.P.M., 30
Royal Commission on Lotteries,
95
Royal Mail Steam Packet
Company, 108
Rutherford,Alderman A. 54, 60

S
St. Anne's Ward, 37, 148, 154,
155, 159
St. Domingo Ward, 166
St. Domingo's Pit, 167
St. George's Plateau, 179
St. Helens, 46
Salvation Army, 83
Salvidge, Archibald, 113, 114
Sandhills Ward, 155
Saville, John, 146
Scotland Constituency, 149
Scotland, North, Ward, 155
Scotland Road, 121, 155
Scotland, South, Ward, 155, 161
Seafarers, 20
Seamen's Union, 27, 31, 140, 141
Sectarianism, Religious, 114, 116
Sefton, Earl of, 109, 110, 114
Sefton Park, 111
Sexton, James, 140, 154
Shop Assistants' Union, 134, 142
Shute, John, 160
Silverman, Sidney, 153, 154-5,
159-60
Snowden, Philip, 146
Social Security Bill (1989), 205

South East, The, 133
Spanish Civil War, 168
Springwood, 51
S.S. *Scottish Prince*, 18
Stadium, Liverpool, 168, 169-72
Stalin, Joseph, 180
"Standstill" Act (1935), 81, 159,
195
State, 10,66
State Medical Services Ass, 46
Strikes – Birkenhead Dockers
(1934), 141
– British Enka Artificial Silk
Works, Aintree (1934), 142
– Cinema Projectionists (1930),
126
– Donegal Tweed Co. (1934), 142f
– Howard, Ford & Co., Woolton
(1935), 142
– Liverpool Dockers (1934), 126
– London Busmen (1937), 137
– Pilkingtons (1933), 142
– Princes' Dock (1933), 141
– Stanley Cattle Market (1933),
142
– Walker's Dairies (1934), 142

T
Tailors and Garment Workers
Union, 142f
Tate and Lyle's, 27, 125
Tebbit, Norman, 203
Tenants Defence League, 52
Thatcher, Margaret, 203
Third International, 180
Thomas, J.H., 146
Trade Union Movement, 119,
132f, 168, 178
Trade Unions, Amalgamation of,
119